MW00342624

FcL

Sport in the American West

Jorge Iber, series editor

Also in the series

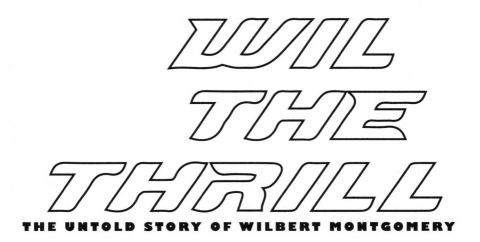

WIL THE THRILL

THE UNTOLD STORY OF WILBERT MONTGOMERY

EDWARD J. ROBINSON

FOREWORD BY RAY DIDINGER

Texas Tech University Press

Copyright © 2013 by Edward J. Robinson

Unless otherwise credited, photographs courtesy Abilene Christian University.

This book is typeset in Minion Pro. The paper used in this book meets the minimum requirements of ANSI/NISO Z39.48–1992 (R1997). ∞

Designed by Kasey McBeath
Cover photograph courtesy Abilene Christian University

Library of Congress Cataloging-in-Publication Data
Robinson, Edward J.
    Wil the thrill : the untold story of Wilbert Montgomery / Edward J. Robinson; foreword by Ray Didinger.
        pages cm. — (Sport in the American west)
    Summary: "The story of Wilbert Montgomery, one of the first African Americans to play football for then Abilene Christian College in Texas; Montgomery later went on to a successful NFL career as player and coach"— Provided by publisher.
    Includes bibliographical references and index.
    ISBN 978-0-89672-847-9 (hardback) — ISBN 978-0-89672-848-6 (e-book) 1. Montgomery, Wilbert. 2. Football players—United States—Biography. 3. Football coaches—United States—Biography. 4. African American football players—Biography. 5. African American football coaches—Biography. I. Title.
    GV939.M593R64 2013
    796.332092—dc23
    [B]   2013022780

13 14 15 16 17 18 19 20 21 / 9 8 7 6 5 4 3 2 1

Texas Tech University Press
Box 41037 | Lubbock, Texas 79409-1037 USA
800.832.4042 | ttup@ttu.edu | www.ttupress.org

To the memory of Gladys Montgomery,
the heart and soul of the Montgomery family,

and to John C. Whitley,
a forgotten trailblazer in African American Churches of Christ

Contents

Illustrations

Foreword

Wilbert Montgomery arrived in Philadelphia in 1977, his eyes fixed on his shoe tops, his voice turned down to a Sunday school whisper. He was painfully shy and not at all sure he belonged in an NFL training camp.

The Philadelphia Eagles selected him in the sixth round of the draft, the 154th player chosen overall. He scored seventy-six touchdowns at Abilene Christian University—an NCAA record—but he missed eleven games in his final two seasons due to various injuries. Most pro scouts felt he was too brittle to last in the NFL, but the Eagles figured that that far down in the draft they had nothing to lose.

He was scared of the big city, scared of pro football, and—most of all—scared of Dick Vermeil, the coach whose piercing voice was everywhere on the practice field. He was going to leave camp one night but his roommate, Cleveland Franklin, talked him out of it. He felt certain it was only a matter of time before he was released. He kept a towel under his door so the coaches could not slide the pink slip into his room.

"Wilbert was insecure, like most rookies, but everyone else in camp recognized his talent," said Ron Jaworski, who quarterbacked that Eagles team. "He had that great vision, the ability to cut back and make something out of nothing. He ran hard, blocked, and caught the ball well. He had everything. The only thing he lacked was confidence."

Montgomery spent his rookie year playing mostly on special teams, and he led the NFC with a 26.9-yard average on kickoff returns. The Eagles weren't very good that year, but in the final week of the season Vermeil gave Montgomery his first start at halfback. It was a cold, rainy December day and Montgomery slashed through the New York Jets for 103 yards and scored two touchdowns in a 27–0 victory.

Jim Brown, the Hall of Fame running back, was doing color commentary on the game. As he left the broadcast booth, Brown said to no one in particular, "That number 31 is a special player. Where have they been hiding him?" I was walking next to Brown when he said it. I relayed the comment to Montgomery in the locker room.

"Jim Brown said that?" Montgomery said, his eyes widening.

"Yeah, he did."

"Wow."

In 1978, he became the team's featured back and gained 1,220 yards on 259 carries, a 4.7-yard average, and scored nine touchdowns. That was the beginning of a four-year run during which Montgomery was the focal point of the Eagles' offense and earned a permanent place in Philadelphia sports history.

He played a total of eight seasons with the Eagles and finished as the team's all-time leader in rushing attempts (1,465) and yards (6,538), surpassing the great Steve Van Buren. Montgomery set the club record for rushing yards in a season with 1,512 yards in 1979. He was the first player in team history to rush for more than 1,000 yards in three different seasons.

Montgomery broke Van Buren's career rushing record in a September 1984 game against Minnesota. At his request, the Eagles did not stop the game to acknowledge his accomplishment. They flashed the news on the scoreboard and the referee handed him the football, but he flipped it to the equipment manager and returned to the huddle. There was no curtain call, no prolonged ovation. That was not his style.

"I wasn't comfortable when everyone made me the center of attention, when I knew the guys opening the holes were just as responsible for what we were doing," Montgomery said. "I didn't feel right, getting all the glory. I'd rather not get any. It's a team game. I'm just one man."

Montgomery was similar to Van Buren in his modesty and approach to the game. Neither man cared about individual statistics; they cared only about helping the team win. Both played through injuries that would have sidelined other backs. That was especially true in the 1981 NFC Championship game when Montgomery played despite having a badly bruised hip and strained knee.

That day, playing in below-zero wind chill against a Dallas defense that had not allowed an opponent to rush for more than 100 yards in twenty-nine consecutive postseason games, Montgomery carried the ball twenty-six times for 194 yards, just two yards short of Van Buren's record for a league championship game set in 1949 against the Los Angeles Rams.

The image is forever frozen in the minds of Eagles fans: Montgomery taking a handoff from Jaworski; starting left, then veering sharply to the right; cutting behind the blocks of center Guy Morriss, guard Woody Peoples, and tackle Jerry Sisemore; finding a crease in the Dallas defense; and racing 42 yards to the end zone. It was the Eagles' second play from scrimmage and it lit the emotional fire of his team and the entire city. The day ended with the Eagles celebrating an NFC title and a trip to Super Bowl XV.

"He's not real big," Morriss said of Montgomery, "but he's got one huge heart."

And in Philadelphia, he left one huge legacy.

Ray Didinger

Acknowledgments

I grew up a passionate Dallas Cowboy fan, but I have long since mellowed. Running backs such as the late Walter Payton of the Chicago Bears, Terry Metcalf of the St. Louis Cardinals, and Wilbert Montgomery of the Philadelphia Eagles—perennial rivals and conference foes of the Cowboys—taught me to appreciate gifted athletes even if they played for opposing teams. Montgomery's relative obscurity particularly intrigued me, and my exploration of his journey from Mississippi to Texas and on to Pennsylvania only deepened my admiration for him. Montgomery's natural ability combined with his grit and spirit of sacrifice empowered his rise from poverty and obscurity to the national athletic scene. All this seemed a story that needed telling. Yet Montgomery would be first to point out that his athletic pilgrimage was no solo trip, since he had many tutors, cheerleaders, and supporters along the way.

The same holds true for me in writing this book, which would have been impossible had it not been for assistance from many people. Librarians at both Abilene Christian University and Southwestern Christian College helped me track down important sources. Wilbert Montgomery's high school coach Gary Dempsey welcomed me into his home in Mississippi on two different occasions and answered many follow-up questions by telephone other times. Former Abilene Christian University coach and athletic director Wally Bullington did the same and more. He graciously retrieved for me the telephone numbers of several of his former players and made it possible for me to contact some of them for interviews. Through his assistances I was able to conduct interviews with the following people: Odis Dolton, Addie Felts, Ricky Felts, Ove Johansson, Wilbert Montgomery, Hubert Pickett, Randy Scott, Bob Strader, and Greg Stirman. Former ACU professors and alumni—including Terry Childers, Ron Hadfield, Charles Hodge, David Merrell, Jack Reese, John C. Whitley, Otis Wright, and his sister Rena Wright—offered me their own perspectives on Wilbert Montgomery. Derron Montgomery, Wilbert's talented son, underscored his love and appreciation for his dad, and he helped me to understand what it was like to have a renowned and reputable father. Patrick M. Gleason, public relations manager for the Baltimore Ravens, helped me secure interviews with three of Wilbert Montgomery's current protégés, Le'Ron McClain, Willis McGahee, and Ray Rice. I also express my heartfelt gratitude to Don and Kay Williams for funding a research trip to Mississippi. These individuals were in many ways my cheerleaders, since after each interview I felt inspired to plug away at this work.

Special thanks go to Texas Tech University Press editors Jorge Iber and Judith Keeling for believing in this project, and to copyeditor Dawn Ollila. John L. Robinson, a retired professor from ACU, helped me smooth out the rough edges of this manuscript. Thanks again, John. And, of course, without my wife and three daughters—my most important cheerleaders—this book could not have been written. I dedicate this book to the memory of Wilbert Montgomery's loving mother, Gladys, and to John C. Whitley, the first African American professor at ACU, whose work and legacy have been virtually forgotten.

WIL
THE
THRILL

Prologue:
"Just Unreal—Barely Human"

On a sultry September night, nine thousand boisterous fans packed Kays Stadium in Jonesboro, Arkansas, to cheer on their Arkansas State University (ASU) Indians against the Abilene Christian College (ACC) Wildcats from Abilene, Texas. Enthusiasm spurred on the crowd as the host team jumped out to a 7–0 lead after a Wildcat fumble. On the next series, Wilbert Montgomery, a freshman running back from Greenville, Mississippi, trotted onto the field, broke the huddle, and then caught a soft pass from senior quarterback Clint Longley. Slashing and dashing through Indian defenders, Montgomery scored his first collegiate touchdown in his first game the first time he touched the football. Sports writer Mark McDonald described the freshman's dazzling run:

> The 5-11, 185-pound tailback darted forward, cut to the sideline, outran his blocking and zipped into the Arkansas State secondary. Two red-shirted defenders closed on him and poised to make the tackle—that was never to be. The two Indians dived at Montgomery almost simultaneously, but the runner was not where he was supposed to be. The two tacklers crashed together in a Keystone Cops tangle of arms, legs and shoulder pads, and Montgomery flitted away from them and glided 39 yards for a touchdown.[1]

Hubert Pickett, then ACC's sophomore fullback, recalled Montgomery's first collegiate score as an "awesome run," confessing, "That's when we realized we had something special."[2] By season's end Montgomery had amassed a startling thirty-one rushing touchdowns, then a National Collegiate Athletic Association (NCAA) record. Later that season an awed East Texas State University (ETSU) scout called Montgomery "barely human," an opinion echoed by an assistant coach for the Stephen F. Austin (SFA) Lumberjacks, after Montgomery tallied six touchdowns against them, describing the ACC running back as "just unreal—barely human." Reflecting on ACC's 1973 national championship season, an equally impressed Gil Steinke, head coach for the Texas A&I Javelinas, added a humorous touch: "I think teams could have played with them if it hadn't been for Montgomery. Man, he made defensive players look like old men chasing a jackrabbit."[3]

The phrase "barely human" might be viewed two ways. Opposing coaches intended the remarks as compliments, highlighting Wilbert Montgomery's amazing athletic skill and power. In short, the Mississippi Delta product was virtually superhuman. But the phrase can also be construed as suggesting (wrongfully) that he was essentially subhuman. Throughout the twentieth century, anthropologists and physical educators debated the notion of black athletic superiority, some arguing that African American athletes enjoyed an innate superiority to their white counterparts owed to their experience in chattel enslavement and their supposed evolutionary proximity to beasts in the jungle. Even though African American athletes ran faster, jumped higher, and hit harder than their white competitors, white people still considered blacks to be intellectually inferior, and thus subhuman.[4]

Some physical educators and physicians viewed racial differences as the primary cause of black athletic dominance. After examining fifty-one white and fifty-one black students at the State University of Iowa, physical educator Eleanor Metheny concluded in 1939 that since African Americans had longer hands and forearms than whites, they excelled in sprinting and jumping contests, but faltered in running long distances. In the 1960s, James M. Tanner, a medical doctor from Britain, expanded on Metheny's theories and insisted that although African American athletes dominated sprints, the long jump, and the high jump, they fizzled out in marathons. In essence, black athletes possessed "great speed but little stamina."[5] In recent years, however, African distance runners have disproved the notion of "little stamina."

Other sports scientists and scholars have refused to attribute racial and physical differences to black athletic success. Thomas K. Cureton, a physical education professor at the University of Illinois, pointed out that black Americans bested white competitors because of "motivation" and "social goals." Harold Edward "Red" Grange, a star halfback for both the University of Illinois and the Chicago Bears, remembered competing with African Americans in his Wheaton, Illinois, neighborhood, and called them "great athletes" who "never had the opportunity." John Wooden, the legendary basketball coach of the University of California, Los Angeles (UCLA), Bruins, similarly observed, "I think he [the black athlete] has just a little more ambition to excel in sports because there aren't enough other avenues open to him." Sports sociologist Harry Edwards similarly argued that black youths' preoccupation with sports had nothing to do with intellectual incompetence; instead, social restrictions forced African Americans to channel their energies into athletic competition.[6]

African American athletes themselves understood the debate swirling around their athletic prowess. Warren McVea, the first black footballer at the University of Houston, expressed rage that whites generally presumed that talented African American athletes were stupid. "No matter what you do out there on the football field," McVea fussed, "you know that white players are going to be thinking two things: that you're some kind of superhuman because you're black and that you're dumb."[7] Jerry LeVias, the first black football player at Southern Methodist University (SMU), knew that his athleticism helped open the door for him in Dallas, stating frankly, "If I weren't supernigger, I wouldn't be here." Wilbert Montgomery attributed his own fancy footwork on the football field to constant practice. After amassing eighty-six all-purpose yards and two touchdowns against powerhouse Texas A&I (now Texas A&M University–Kingsville) University, he commented that as an adolescent he often put old tires in the street and ran through them "without breaking stride." That Montgomery placed worn-out tires in the streets of his neighborhood in Greenville, Mississippi, to enhance his agility suggests that circumstances influenced his decision to focus on football instead of other sports. Impoverished black Americans had more ready access to old tires than to expensive golf clubs and tennis rackets. Thus, sports historian David K. Wiggins has fittingly concluded, "If blacks place a decided premium on physical virtuosity through sport, as many people have claimed, it is caused more by their particular station in life than by any hereditary factors."[8]

Even though the debate over black athletic superiority raged throughout the twentieth century, white football coaches across the country came to realize the value of African American athletes. After the Southwest Conference (SWC) had become fully integrated in 1970, former Texas Christian University (TCU) coach Fred Taylor confessed, "My God, where would you be without the black athletes? You go to looking back and you say, 'How in the hell did we ever have a league without black players?'"[9] Coach Taylor without question spoke for coaches in the Lone Star Conference (LSC) as well, since they clearly had never encountered an athlete quite like Wilbert Montgomery, a young black man with incredible skill and natural ability. Notwithstanding his extraordinary gridiron feats, Montgomery's eventful story has been largely ignored, perhaps because he failed to showcase his athleticism at the Division I NCAA level, never won the Heisman Trophy, and came short of winning a Super Bowl ring as a professional football player with the Philadelphia Eagles.

A number of sports historians have highlighted the significance of athletic competition in breaking down racial barriers. Sports journalist Frank Fitzpatrick has argued that the 1966 national championship basketball game between Texas Western College (now the University of Texas at El Paso) and the University of Kentucky altered forever American sports as well as American society. Don Haskins, Texas Western's coach, started five black players against the traditional and all-white powerhouse the Kentucky Wildcats. The Miners from El Paso upset Kentucky, 72–65, and Fitzpatrick insisted the game signaled the "end of athletic segregation" in that many white people realized that they were "wrong about the capabilities of black basketball players. About Catholicism. About a lot of things."[10]

For Fitzpatrick the year 1966 marked a turning point in American sports, but for sports analyst William C. Rhoden, 1970 stood out as the pivotal year. On September 12, 1970, football fans across America witnessed Sam "Bam" Cunningham, running back for the University of Southern California Trojans, plow through Bear Bryant's Alabama Crimson Tide defense. A black 6'3", 245-pound sophomore, Cunningham rushed for 135 yards on eleven carries and scored two touchdowns as the Trojans crushed the Crimson Tide, 42–21. "Cunningham would be called the catalyst for integration in the South," Rhoden asserted, "and the game drove home the point that George Wallace's June 1963 proclamation—'Segregation now, segregation tomorrow, segregation forever'—would have to be modified to accommodate the great black athlete."[11]

While Fitzpatrick and Rhoden correctly highlight the years 1966 and 1970 as transformative times in American sports, this book holds that the untold story of Wilbert Montgomery both complements and complicates the narrative of American athletics. This work tells the forgotten tale of Montgomery, a young black athlete from the Mississippi Delta who left the Magnolia State in 1973, found a warm and cordial reception at an overwhelmingly white Christian college in West Texas, and left an indelible mark as a student-athlete there and beyond. It lends credence to researcher Lane Demas's thesis that African American college athletes "played a fundamental role in contesting and reshaping the broader social struggle" across twentieth-century America. "Black college football players," Demas contends, "helped their schools make headlines throughout the twentieth century, especially after World War II. A few were well known around the country, but most were not."[12] African American athletes such as Montgomery helped elevate their schools to national prominence and simultaneously contested the racist attitudes of some of their white admirers. Montgomery's remarkable story is singular in that it encompasses the complex intersection of race, sports, and religion.

The athletic pilgrimage of Wilbert Montgomery was not altogether unique, however. In 1948 Bill Garrett became the first African American in Big Ten basketball, playing for the Indiana Hoosiers at guard for three years.[13] Unlike in the North where basketball was king, football reigned across the South. Segregation, however, barred black southerners from white colleges and universities, forcing many gifted African American athletes to take their talents to northern or western cities. In the 1930s, Oze Simmons left the Lone Star State to play football at the University of Iowa. In 1960 Charles Taylor, a speedy receiver from Grand Prairie, Texas, played collegiate ball for the Arizona State Sun Devils before a successful career with the Washington Redskins. The following year Junior Coffey, another native Texan, relocated to Washington State to compete for the Washington Huskies before being drafted by the Atlanta Falcons. In 1963 Charles "Bubba" Smith, a fierce defensive tackle from Beaumont, Texas, chose to enroll at Michigan State University.[14]

The next year Don Chaney, Elvin Hayes, and Warren McVea shook up sports in the Deep South by enrolling at the University of Houston, knocking what historian Katherine Lopez has called a "clear dent in the pervasive racism of the South."[15] In 1965 John Westbrook, a native of Groesbeck, Texas, entered Baylor University and became the first black athlete to play in an SWC football game. Around the same time, Jerry LeVias signed a letter of intent to play football at SMU. Religious institutions such as SMU, Texas Christian University (TCU), and Baylor helped "break the ice" of racial segregation for other powerhouse programs such as the University of Texas and University of Arkansas, the last two SWC schools to welcome African American football players.[16]

After prodding from courageous black preachers such as R. N. Hogan and scrupulous white leaders such as Carl Spain, white Church of Christ colleges began admitting African American students in the early 1960s. In 1962 Billy Curl and Larry Bonner became the first black undergraduate students at ACC. Curl, a native of Nacogdoches, Texas, and a graduate of Southwestern Christian College (SWCC), remembered it as a time of uncertainty. "I had no idea what I was getting myself into," he recalled. "I was on a mission just to get an education." Despite being spurned by some ACC students and faculty members, others befriended him and helped him complete his degree.[17] Six years later Henry Willis transferred from Howard County Junior College to play basketball at ACC, becoming the first black scholarship athlete at ACC.[18] Thus, when Wilbert Montgomery enrolled at ACC in 1973, he was among a handful of black student athletes there. Unlike John Westbrook of Baylor University and Jerry LeVias of SMU, who showcased their talents within the confines of Texas at church-related schools on a Division I level, Montgomery chose to journey 573 miles from his hometown in Greenville, Mississippi, to play collegiate football at a Division II Christian school in West Texas. Stories of African American athletes who successfully integrated Division I college football programs abound; however, accounts of black athletes who toppled lingering racial barriers at predominantly white and smaller Christian college campuses are few.

Furthermore, whereas running backs "Pistol" Pete Pedro, "Mercury" Morris, and Duane Thomas dazzled fans at West Texas State (now West Texas A&M) University in Canyon in the 1960s, none of them left the mark on West Texas athletics that Wilbert Montgomery did. Pedro, a diminutive 5'7", 160-pound running back, played two seasons at Trinidad State Junior College in Colorado before amassing 2,167 yards and thirty-three touchdowns for the Buffs from 1960 to 1962. Following in Pedro's path, Morris, a native of Pennsylvania, enrolled at West Texas State University and had a stellar four-year career before signing with the Miami Dolphins in 1969. Thomas, a native of Dallas, Texas, played with Morris in Canyon before being drafted by the Dallas Cowboys in 1970.[19] West Texans, then, were familiar with standout black athletes, but Montgomery remained in a class by himself.

John C. Stevens, a World War II combat veteran and ACC's president from 1969 to 1981, steered the college to university status in 1976. In his 1998 book on the history and significance of Abilene Christian University (ACU), Stevens proudly labeled the West Texas school "no ordinary university" and a "city set on a hill."[20] Although many adept administrators, learned professors, accomplished students, and generous donors have contributed to ACU's longevity and prosperity, I posit that black athletes like Wilbert Montgomery helped whites at both the university and surrounding communities to become more appreciative and accepting of black people in general and of African American student-athletes in particular. Montgomery's athletic exploits, which football-mad West Texans had never before seen, helped make ACU an extraordinary university as ACU profoundly shaped Montgomery and Montgomery indelibly stamped the ACU community. In the 1970s Montgomery helped catapult ACU to further national prominence by garnering the attention of professional scouts and prominent sports writers.

Wilbert Montgomery followed a trail already blazed by several other outstanding ACC athletes, including 1940s running back V. T. Smith, 1950s Olympic champion Bobby Morrow, 1960s star hurdler Earl Young, and late 1960s and early 1970s star quarterback Jim Lindsey. Yet these earlier athletes achieved their impressive feats when competition was mostly between white athletes and when the institution was smaller and lesser known. Montgomery's tenure in Abilene occurred when the school was transitioning to university status, when competition was becoming stiffer and less restricted, and when college football was blossoming into a national, prime time sport. Montgomery's presence often attracted 12,000 to 15,000 spectators to home football games, and he also swayed several other African American student-athletes to enroll there. After Montgomery's departure, world-renowned pole-vaulter Billy Olson continued the tradition of garnering national attention for ACU athletics.

Montgomery's athletic career at ACU and beyond strikingly parallels those of other notable black athletes. Jackie Robinson and Willie Mays helped demolish racial barriers in Major League Baseball. Jonathan Eig has written that Robinson "proved that black Americans had been held back not by their inferiority but by systematic discrimination. And he proved it not with printed words or arguments declaimed before a judge. He proved it with deeds."[21] James "Poo" Johnson, a close friend of Willie Mays, remarked, "Instead of stepping out and marching, [Mays] was changing attitudes one person at a time"; another admirer claimed that the presence of African Americans in professional baseball "*unbigoted* some bigots."[22]

Marcus Dupree, a black teenager from Philadelphia, Mississippi, helped unite a racially torn community, where in 1964 Klansmen had brutally murdered three civil rights workers, James Chaney, Andrew Goodman, and Michael Schwerner. By the early 1980s, Dupree had emerged as the most sought after football player in the nation. His ability and popularity helped quell racial tension in northeast Mississippi and brought positive national attention to an area that had seemed irreparably scarred. Marty Stuart, a Philadelphia resident, commented that Dupree has "made for better relationships in *this* town. Marcus Dupree shows it depends on the individual, not the color of the skin. We had a bad name. . . . But Marcus Dupree helped everything around here." Cella Conner, Dupree's mother, confessed that many outsiders viewed Mississippi as backward, "fifty years behind the times." She added that "I'd like to think my sons had something to do in helping bring whites and blacks closer together."[23]

John C. Whitley, the first African American professor at Abilene Christian College, recently pointed out that Wilbert Montgomery was "like Jackie Robinson." Montgomery's "greatest contribution," according to Whitley, was his humility, patience, and determination to use his gift. When he had the opportunity to shine, he made it possible "by not fussing." After he gained local attention and national acclaim, he never got a "big head." He was a "super guy, but never braggadocio." Bob Strader, a defensive back on ACC's 1973 championship team, recently compared Montgomery's speed, strength, balance, and ability to change direction swiftly to Detroit Lions running back Reggie Bush. Both Whitley and Strader concluded that the combination of his natural talent and humble disposition enabled Montgomery to improve race relations at a Christian college in West Texas and beyond.[24]

I maintain that even though Wilbert Montgomery never attained the national fame of a Jackie Robinson or a Willie Mays, through athletics he made a marked difference in race relations in West Texas. Montgomery's experiences on a mostly white college campus led to an influx of African American students, especially student-athletes from the Mississippi Delta, to ACC and raised levels of racial understanding and acceptance in the broader West Texas community.

Wil the Thrill consists of nine chapters in three sections. Chapter 1 probes Wilbert Montgomery's family and background, assessing the stabilizing forces in his sometimes chaotic world and rehearsing his rise as a highly touted high school athlete from the Magnolia State. The next chapter appraises his two-year gridiron career with the Greenville High Hornets, and chapter 3 explores his courageous and controversial decision to withdraw from the predominantly black Jackson State College (JSC) in Jackson, Mississippi, and enroll at the mostly white ACC in Abilene, Texas. Chapter 4 recounts ACC's 1973 championship season and Montgomery's freshman year as an ACC Wildcat. Chapters 5 through 7 assess the successes and struggles Montgomery encountered during his sophomore, junior, and senior years, and the last two chapters examine Montgomery's ascendancy to the National Football League with the Philadelphia Eagles—where he earned the nickname "Wil the Thrill"—as well as his transition from a player to his role as mentor and running backs coach.

Wilbert Montgomery, a black teenager from the Mississippi Delta, escaped to West Texas and effected a profound and enduring difference there. His story bears witness that social change emanated not always from preachers, politicians, and protesters; instead, sometimes unassuming young people from ordinary backgrounds but with extraordinary abilities made their world better by quietly going about their daily tasks. Such neglected stories are well worth the telling.

Part I

Wilbert Montgomery in
the Mississippi Delta, 1954–1972

Chapter 1

Rocks in a Weary Land: The Education of Wilbert Montgomery

I understand that fellow [Vince] Lombardi was a great motivator, but he couldn't teach my Mama anything.

Earl Campbell (quoted in Sam Blair, *Earl Campbell: The Driving Force*, 13)

The 1950s, the South, it was a strange trip. Back then, it was wise to avoid entire states. Stay way the fuck away from Mississippi. In the South you had to worry for your life, and you worried not about so-called criminals, but the government.

Jim Brown (quoted in Jim Brown and Steve Delsohn, *Out of Bounds,* 54)

On May 17, 1954, the United State Supreme Court handed down the *Brown v. Board of Education* decision, ruling that segregated schools "are inherently unequal."[1] The historic decision enthused most African Americans, but enraged southern whites, who vowed to contest and protest what they deemed to be a violation of their states' rights.[2] Four months later Roosevelt and Gladys Montgomery welcomed a baby boy, Wilbert, into their home in Cleveland, Mississippi—located in the Mississippi Delta, which one historian has called "the most southern place on earth."[3] Stark economic disparity between elite whites and impoverished blacks in the Delta preserved "antebellum conditions."[4] Such horrific conditions prompted one black woman in Mississippi to exclaim, "Mississippi is awful. All the important things Negroes can't do."[5]

In the 1950s and 1960s, Wilbert Montgomery's childhood and adolescent years, black Mississippians lived a precarious existence. On May 7, 1955, Reverend George Lee met a violent death in Belzoni, Mississippi, for leading a voter registration drive. On August 13, 1955, sixty-three-year-old World War II veteran Lamar Smith was fatally shot on the courthouse lawn in Brookhaven, Mississippi, for organizing black voters. Two weeks later, Roy Bryant and J. W. Milan, white store clerks in Money, Mississippi, brutally murdered Emmett L. Till, a fourteen-year-old black youth from Chicago. The slaughter of Till made him the "sacrificial lamb" of the civil rights movement. On April 25, 1959, a white woman in Poplarville, Mississippi, accused Mack Charles Parker, a black army veteran, of rape. Shortly before Parker's trial, an angry white mob dragged him from his jail cell, beat him, shot him to death, and tossed his body into the Pearl River. On April 9, 1962, a white police officer in Taylorsville, Mississippi, shot and killed Roman Ducksworth Jr., a military police officer, "because he insisted on his rights to sit where he chose on a bus." On June 12, 1963, Byron De La Beckwith, a charter member of the White Citizens' Council, shot and killed Medgar Evers, a World War II veteran and an NAACP field secretary for the Magnolia State. In the "freedom summer" of 1964, Klansmen conspired and murdered three civil rights workers, James Chaney, Andrew Goodman, and Michael Schwerner, in Philadelphia, Mississippi.[6] These bloody events inspired one black resident of Greenville, Mississippi, to "get my famaly [sic] out of this cursed South land down here a Negro man is not good as a white man's dog."[7] This was the tumultuous world in which young Wilbert Montgomery lived and moved.

Many African Americans in Mississippi shared the foregoing sentiment, voicing displeasure of their mistreatment by their white counterparts with their feet. Between 1910 and 1960, more than 900,000 blacks exited the Magnolia State because they sought better social conditions and better economic opportunities—and because they yearned to feel, in the words of writer Richard Wright, "the warmth of other suns."[8] Despite the racist and violent forces driving many blacks out of Mississippi, the Montgomery family chose to stay and fight for their dignity and rights. They fought not by marching with protesters or by signing and disseminating petitions; instead, they helped vanquish racial discrimination by slashing through tacklers on the gridiron.

Like many in his social and racial milieu, Wilbert Montgomery grew up in an unstable and impoverished family. His father, Roosevelt, virtually abandoned Wilbert and his eleven siblings. In 1975 when Abilene sports writer Art Lawler interviewed Wilbert, his brother Cleotha, and four other black athletes from the Mississippi Delta, he noted that the young men did not highly regard their fathers. A talkative Cleotha said, "We saw our dad about three years ago. He gets around. He calls one time from one state, the next time from some other state. He keeps moving."[9] Wilbert recently acknowledged that his father was not "involved" in their lives.[10] Roosevelt Montgomery was both unsettled and irresponsible; therefore, the burden of childrearing fell on the shoulders of Wilbert's mother and grandparents, who raised him and his siblings in Greenville. This extended family arrangement gave the Montgomery siblings stability amid a chaotic and turbulent environment. More specifically, three rocks, or stabilizing forces, made the difference in Wilbert's life.

Like many other gifted athletes who grew up without responsible fathers, such as Jackie Robinson and Jim Brown[11], Wilbert Montgomery and his family were poverty stricken. Star running back Earl Campbell's father died when Earl was eleven, leaving his mother, Ann, with the sole responsibility of taking care of ten children. Campbell recalled that they were "poor," but "rich in a lot of ways."[12] What held true for the Campbell family in East Texas proved equally true for the Montgomerys in the Mississippi Delta. They were impoverished yet wealthy—poor in money and material resources, but rich in terms of the love, respect, and natural athletic talent they possessed.

A caring and nurturing woman, Gladys Montgomery was extremely protective of her family. Had her wishes prevailed, her sons would have never played football. Gladys called the game "craziness," nothing but "fools ripping each other's arms and legs off." After her oldest son, Alfred, separated both shoulders playing junior college football, Mrs. Montgomery vowed that her sons would never "play football again." Aware of his mother's vow, Wilbert was heartbroken because he wanted to play football for the Greenville High Hornets. Consequently, he resorted to deception. "I got a girl in my class to forge my mother's signature," Wilbert recalled, "and I made all my friends promise they wouldn't tell her what was going on." After football practice Wilbert justified his tardiness by claiming to be at a friend's house. On Friday nights he explained his lateness, saying "Momma, I'm goin' out for a while. I'll be home by 10:30." If he came home limping, Wilbert told her that he was with friends "fooling around."[13] The same deception Wilbert practiced at home spilled over onto the football field, as he often outran, outcut, and outwitted bigger players. "The boys are just a little bigger that's all," explained Wilbert. "You just got to make those big guys over-pursue, so you can cut back."[14]

Wilbert Montgomery could not keep his personal secrets under wraps for long in Greenville, Mississippi, however. As his high school statistics mushroomed, the local newspaper *Delta Democrat-Times* took notice and touted him as both a defensive and offensive standout. To solve the problem of his growing popularity, Wilbert ripped out the sports page every night and stashed it at his grandfather's house so that his mother would not learn of his playing football. The guilt of hiding the truth from his mother overwhelmed Wilbert, and eventually forced him to come clean. After being honest with his mother about playing high school football, Gladys said, "I know football must have meant a whole lot to him, 'cause he never lied to me before." Mrs. Montgomery eventually learned to accept her seven sons' (Alfred, Wilbert, Cleotha, Jerry, Leonard, John, and Willie) desire to play football, but she regretted that all of them wanted to be running backs. "Why do they all have to play a position," she deplored, "where they get tackled on every play? Out of seven boys, wouldn't you think I'd have one punter? Even a quarterback wouldn't be so bad."[15]

Gladys' soft spot for Wilbert made it difficult for her to watch his games with the Philadelphia Eagles, especially when he was tackled. "That's my Wilbert down there," she screamed, "with all those giants jumping on top of him." "Oh, Wilbert," she added, "why couldn't you have been better in basketball?" In middle of the 1978 season, Wilbert suffered a badly sprained knee and ankle. Stretched out on a table in the Eagles' locker room, his legs sealed with "two balloon-like, yellow hip boots" pumping cold water against his aching muscles, Wilbert smiled and thought about his mother: "If my mother could see me now. All banged up, hooked up to this machine. She'd die, I swear."[16]

Gladys Montgomery seemed to be closer to Wilbert than to all her other children. She remembered Wilbert clinging to her apron as a child, hanging around the house as an adolescent, and as a teenager sitting with her while she prepared dinner. Gladys recalled the pain when Wilbert went off to college in Abilene, Texas, exclaiming, "Lord, how the two of us cried." Wilbert was a mama's boy who was painfully shy. Mrs. Montgomery never could envision her favorite as a "big celebrity." "What does he say," she asked, "to all those reporters, anyway? Poor child, he must be scared half to death."[17] Wilbert's shyness became more and more conspicuous as he excelled in the college and professional ranks. The more fame and notoriety pursued him; the more he fled. His agent, Bob MacDonald, often encouraged him "to cash in" on his popularity and the Philadelphia's Eagles' success by attending banquets. Yet Wilbert refused to participate. "Wilbert is a very quiet type kid," explained MacDonald. "He really doesn't want to make any appearances. So there's no use pushing somebody into something they don't want to do."[18] The shyness he exhibited during his childhood stayed with him through much of his adult life.

Not only did Wilbert Montgomery's mother, Gladys, prove to be a source of stability for Wilbert and his siblings, his grandfather Andrew Williams was also a pillar that sustained him as he grew up in the Mississippi Delta. Wilbert's father neglected him, but his grandfather taught him how to be a man. Wilbert said that Andrew Williams was "everything." He supported his family as a field laborer, often overworked and underpaid. He also dabbled in boxing as a hobby. He taught his grandsons how to fight, how to protect themselves, and how to subdue an assailant with one swift and stiff strike.[19]

In addition, Andrew Williams instilled in Wilbert a strong work ethic, which he carried into his adult life. The family of Ron McMullin, Wilbert's neighbor and close friend, operated a bricklaying business, and Wilbert worked during summer months as a bricklayer to buy his own clothes. Hard labor helped him become responsible and self-reliant at an early age. Wilbert's high school coaches immediately noted that Wilbert's work habits and natural ability and quickness compensated for his lack of size. Reflecting on Wilbert's diligence several years later, Fred Washington, a Greenville High School coach, called him an inspiration to young people, pointing out that "Wilbert is someone the kids can identify with. He's not real big. He didn't go to a big school (Jackson State, then Abilene Christian). He just worked his butt off and now he's up there with the Paytons and Dorsetts."[20] Wilbert learned from his diligent grandfather that hard work and perseverance could compensate for one's size, one's background, even one's skin color.

The third rock in Wilbert's young life was Gary Dempsey. A native of

Anguila, Mississippi, Dempsey starred as a versatile athlete at Mississippi State University, where he earned fifteen varsity letters—six in baseball, five in football, and four in basketball. After his sophomore season, he devoted himself solely to baseball. Upon graduating from MSU in 1961, Dempsey played AA and AAA professional baseball in the Los Angeles Dodgers organization, exiting with a lifetime batting average of over .300. In 1970 he became head coach at Greenville High School, a position he held for nine years. Dempsey appointed Albert Paul, a native of Yazoo County and an alumnus of Mississippi State University, as the Hornets' offensive coordinator, and he hired Frederick Adams, a native of Columbus, Georgia, and a graduate of Jackson State College, to coach the defensive line.[21] The appointment of Paul, a white coach, and Adams, a black mentor, was likely designed to help quell racial tensions in Greenville. Two years later, Dempsey hired another black assistant coach, Frank Davis. A native of Port Gibson, Mississippi, and a graduate of Alcorn State College, Davis coached the offensive line. Davis had planned to pursue his master's degree at the University of Southern Mississippi, but he "couldn't pass up the opportunity here."[22]

Shortly after Dempsey assumed GHS's head coaching position, Montgomery began his high school football career, imbibing Dempsey's philosophy of "Don't tell me. Show me." Consequently, throughout Wilbert's athletic career he never boasted and bragged about what he would accomplish on the field. Instead, he simply went out as a quiet leader and performed efficiently from week to week. Even though Wilbert excelled on both sides of the ball, Dempsey believed that Wilbert was a special running back. His greatest asset on the gridiron was his "sixth sense." He knew how "to plant his foot and run."[23]

Wilbert Montgomery, born and reared in "the most southern place on earth," survived and thrived because of the three rocks—Gladys Montgomery, Andrew Williams, and Gary Dempsey—who touched and transformed his life. Abandoned by a derelict father, Wilbert received unconditional love and tenderness from a loving and protective mother. His grandfather transmitted to him the toughness to protect himself as well as a work ethic that he carried into adulthood. His mother and grandfather trusted coach Gary Dempsey, who taught Wilbert to be a silent leader and to do his talking on the field. Wilbert's ability to cut and run on a dime led him out of the Mississippi Delta and eventually to West Texas, where he also left an indelible mark in the hearts and minds of his fans.

The "Montgomery Express": Wilbert and Cleotha Montgomery and the Greenville Hornets

A friend loveth at all times, and a brother is born for adversity.

Proverbs 17:17

[T]he soul of Jonathan was knit with the soul of David, and Jonathan loved him as his own soul.

1 Samuel 18:1

An interviewer once asked Greenville High football coach Gary Dempsey, "Who was the best offensive player you ever coached?" Dempsey quickly responded, "Wilbert Montgomery." Then came the second question, "Who was the best defensive player you ever coached?" Dempsey again replied, "Wilbert Montgomery."[1] Montgomery, waiting to play with his younger brother Cleotha, did not join Dempsey's varsity squad until his junior year.[2] The "Montgomery boys" immediately excelled on both sides of the ball: Wilbert started at tailback and safety, while Cleotha started at both wingback and defensive back. The two brothers led the Greenville Hornets to a state title in 1971 and a co-championship in 1972.

The story of the Montgomery brothers and the Greenville Hornets bears a striking similarity to the 2000 movie *Remember the Titans*, based on the 1971 championship season of the T. C. Williams Titans in Alexandria, Virginia. Herman Boone, portrayed by Denzel Washington, takes over for Bill Yoast, played by Will Patton. The biracial coaching staff and their biracial football team consistently clashed during training camp. Yet after rigorous training and forceful coaxing, racial harmony prevailed among team members. More significantly, the Titans' gridiron success helped engender racial unity in the segregated town of Alexandria. The racial discord in Virginia in the early 1970s was a microcosm of the strife afflicting other southern states.

Just as the T. C. Williams Titans positively influenced race relations in Virginia, the talented Montgomery duo produced a 19–1 record over a two-year period, thereby bringing about greater unity in a racially divided Mississippi Delta community. The Greenville Hornets got off to a good start on the field as Wilbert led his team to a 35–0 rout in the season opener, but racial hostility swirled around the GHS campus and Greenville.[3] Schools in Greenville had been desegregated only in 1970[4], and a year later—when the Montgomery boys launched their high school gridiron careers—racial tension still coursed through the city. Decades of segregation enforced by lynch law had left their cruel marks. Coach Gary Dempsey remembered it as a time with "a lot of tension," a "nerve-racking" experience. "You did not know what was going to happen the next hour," he added.[5] So the coach challenged his players to be part of the "solution," not part of the "problem."[6] Taking Dempsey's challenge to heart, Elliott Williams, GHS's student body president and a speedy black running back, published an article in Greenville's *Delta Democrat-Times*, calling on his classmates to unite. "This is our school, our education, and it affects our lives," pleaded Williams. "Even though many of us did not ask for one high school, we have it. So let's make it our own. WE must have open minds and willingly accept change as a challenge—not a defeat."[7] Greenville football players found themselves fighting battles on and off the field.

An anonymous respondent chided Williams, asserting, "Elliott, there is nothing at GHS that illustrates anything as being black." Writing with a bitter tone, the respondent continued, "Elliott, can you honestly say that your black brothers can learn at GHS?" The anonymous writer clearly felt that desegregation harmed the African American community. "Elliott," he urged, "take a stand as a black man, don't let people infringe upon your black brothers' rights."[8] The exchange between Williams and the respondent underscores the divisiveness that pervaded the African American community during the post–civil rights era. It represents on the one hand those who were optimistic and willing to work toward racial harmony, but on the other hand it signifies that many remained skeptical about integration and were willing to live, learn, and work separately from white people.

The racial tension at GHS evidently inspired Elliott Williams, however. In the Hornets' second game of the season, he racked up 142 yards and two touchdowns in a 12–0 victory over the Caldwell Bobcats.[9] In their third game the Hornets, led by Williams's 90 yards on eleven carries, blanked the Tupelo Green Wave, 7–0.[10] The Hornets then stung the Cleveland Wildcats, 31–7, for their fourth consecutive win—behind Williams's 144 yards, eighteen carries, and two touchdowns.[11]

Greenville traveled next to Meridian to take on the third-ranked Wildcats for their fifth game of the season. With the sharp passing of quarterback David McCraney, the explosive running of Elliott Williams, and the shrewd defensive play of Cleotha Montgomery, the Hornets pummeled the Wildcats, 34–14, before eight thousand avid fans. McCraney completed ten out of twenty-three passes for 207 yards, while Williams, "a speed merchant," tallied 146 yards on eleven carries.[12] Williams scored three more touchdowns in the sixth game of the season, as the Hornets hammered the Corinth Warriors, 36–12, and catapulted to the number-one ranking in the state of Mississippi.[13] The Pine Bluff Zebras from Arkansas then limited Williams to fourteen yards, yet the Hornets still prevailed, 34–12, after quarterback McCraney tossed four touchdown passes, three to receiver Larry Kennedy, and one to wingback Cleotha Montgomery.[14] The homecoming victory over the Zebras guaranteed the Hornets at least a share of the North Division Mississippi title.[15]

Success on the gridiron, however, failed to translate into racial harmony off the field. After the homecoming win over Pine Bluff, James Hodges Jr., a member of the Hornets' football team, lamented that black players had "no place to go celebrate." Hodges's mother then spontaneously invited the entire team to her house on 155 South Delta Street. Two hundred fifty GHS students showed up, but "no whites came, though." Mrs. Hodges pointed out that most students were willing to interact freely with classmates regardless of race, but "parents . . . warp their minds." One black student poignantly captured the conflicting emotions most African American students must have felt: "It makes it kind of sad when we all get forced to go to school together and by some miracle get along fairly well, considering, and then something happens like that beautiful game which left so many of us happy and we can't celebrate together. It's like a wall that came tumbling down when we were there cheering and hollering, and screaming together . . . but it was put right back up again when it came time to go our separate ways."[16] White parents in the Mississippi Delta permitted their sons to compete with black athletes on the gridiron, but they adamantly refused to allow their daughters to mingle with them in social contexts. Fear of sex between white women and black men gripped the minds of many white southerners, prompting them to draw a "floating line" between races in the Deep South. Mississippi racial etiquette at that time confined social equality to the field, keeping intact the time-honored code of white superiority and black inferiority once the game ended. In 1988 Nate Hearne, an African American coach at Permian High School in Odessa, Texas, captured this social disparity well. "We fit as athletes," observed Hearne, "but we really don't fit as a part of society. We know that we're equal as athletes. But once we get off the field we're not equal. When it comes time to play the game, we are a part of it. But after the game, we are not part of it."[17]

The Greenville High football team, however, refused to allow off-the-field tension to deter them from their goal of a state championship. The Hornets' offense amassed 514 yards against the South Vicksburg Greenies to win easily. Elliott Williams carried the ball ten times for 143 yards and two touchdowns; Wilbert Montgomery added 83 yards on eight carries. In their regular season finale against the Greenwood High Bulldogs, the Hornets won in dramatic fashion after the Bulldogs struck for a 14–0 lead before the Hornets came back; Williams scored on a last minute two-point conversion, sealing a 15–14 triumph.[18]

The Hornets' win over Greenwood lifted them into the state championship game against the Callaway Chargers. Ranked number one and number two, the two teams competed in the first-ever Capital Bowl in Jackson, Mississippi. They battled to a 14–14 tie until fullback Hugh Christian kicked a 22-yard game-winning field goal late in the fourth quarter. Running back Elliott Williams led the Hornets with 98 rushing yards on twenty-two carries. Wilbert Montgomery chipped in 50 yards on ten carries, but had a 40-yard touchdown run nullified because a "Hornet failed to have his mouth-piece where it belongs on each play."[19]

The Hornets' championship season generated numerous postseason awards for individual coaches and players. The Big Eight Conference named Gary Dempsey "Coach of the Year."[20] Defensive end Charles Brady, running back Elliott Williams, split end Larry Kennedy, defensive end J. W. Williams, and linebacker Ricky Franklin all represented the Hornets on the North All–Big Eight Team.[21] Even though Wilbert and Cleotha Montgomery contributed substantially to the Hornets' 1971 unblemished season, they received virtually no recognition that year. Yet coach Dempsey knew that the Montgomery duo were athletically gifted and that their presence ensured a bright future for his Hornets.

Following the departure of Elliott Williams for the University of Texas at El Paso, Wilbert Montgomery emerged as the pivotal player for Greenville in 1972. The Hornets' quest for consecutive state championships essentially vanished, however, after the opening 19–14 loss to the Tupelo Golden Wave, as seven penalties and three lost fumbles sealed the Hornets' defeat. Ron McMullin's 41 yards on four carries and Wilbert Montgomery's 74 kickoff return yards stood as bright spots in the Hornets' defeat.[22] Despite the devastating loss, coach Dempsey named Montgomery the Hornets' player of the game, adding, "He's not the talkative type leader. . . . He leads by example and doesn't expect others to do any more than he will do himself."[23]

The Greenville Hornets, led by "the Montgomery Express," bounced back with a 19–14 win over the Pine Bluff Zebras. Wilbert scored the first six points for the Hornets when he, in the words of sports editor Mitch Ariff, "took a delayed pitchout around left from quarterback Bill Hammett, cut inside at about the 25 and then outraced defenders for an 81-yard touchdown gallop." Cleotha performed solidly as well, catching a 30-yard touchdown pass and making the "game-saving tackle."[24] In their fourth game of the season, Wilbert, Cleotha, and Ron McMullin scored two touchdowns each, as the Hornets swept aside the Cleveland Wildcats, 43–15. Wilbert scored on an 85-yard run, McMullin sprinted 94 yards for a touchdown, and Cleotha returned a kickoff 78 yards.[25] The Hornets then improved their record to four wins and one loss after slipping past the Meridian Wildcats, 21–20, as Wilbert paced the Hornets with 83 yards on ten carries, while McMullin gained 83 yards on eight carries.[26]

As the season progressed, Wilbert and Cleotha Montgomery shone even more brightly for Greenville. The brothers helped lead the Hornets to an impressive 14–6 victory over Airline High from Bossier City, Louisiana. "On the opening kickoff and the first play from scrimmage," explained sports writer Mitch Ariff, "the Montgomery boys—Cleotha and Wilbert—gave Hornet fans hope of an easy contest. . . . [T]hey [the fans] wanted nothing like the cliffhanger of a week ago." Wilbert, "equally as good on defense," intercepted Airline quarterback Steve Haynes's pass and returned it 30 yards. Returning to the field as a running back, Wilbert then bewildered the defenders with a dazzling 29-yard touchdown run. "Montgomery had circled left," reported Ariff, "cut inside and then dodged and twisted his way into the end zone on the beautiful run." Although the Hornets held a 14–0 lead at halftime, Airline roared back with a third quarter touchdown. But safety Ron McMullin intercepted a Haynes pass with thirteen seconds left in the game, preserving a 14–6 win.[27]

After enjoying an open week, the Hornets resumed their winning ways by demolishing the Columbus Lee Generals, 43–7. McMullin took the opening kickoff back 90 yards for the first touchdown before an ankle injury sidelined him for the rest of the contest. But Wilbert Montgomery quickly took over and rushed for 97 yards on thirteen carries and two touchdowns.[28] A week later the Hornets spotted the Clarksdale Wildcats a 12–0 lead before Wilbert ignited his team with a pair of brilliant touchdown runs, leading a 22–12 comeback win. Coach Dempsey hailed Wilbert as "one of the best running backs in the state of Mississippi. [He] made a great deal of difference in the final outcome. It seems that with his first TD run, he triggered inspired play by all of our players and from that point on, it was the Hornets' ball game." Montgomery ended the night with 152 yards on fourteen carries and two touchdowns.[29]

Wilbert Montgomery topped off his high school gridiron career with a 34–14 win over archrival Greenwood High, leading the way with 100 yards on twelve carries and two touchdowns.[30] With the win over the Bulldogs, the Hornets grabbed a share of the North Division Big Eight Conference crown with the Clarksdale Wildcats.[31] The Hornets landed four players on the All–Big Eight Conference Team, including defensive lineman Glenn Washington, linebacker Hugh Christian, offensive tackle Jones Redd, and Wilbert Montgomery.[32] Even though the Hornets failed to win the Big Eight crown outright, coach Dempsey considered his 1972 team "better" than his 1971 championship crew.[33]

Wilbert, then, had emerged as a formidable force in 1971, and Gary Dempsey and his coaching staff rode the "Montgomery Express" for two seasons, compiling a 19–1 record. The 1971 Hornet squad was Elliott Williams's team, but the 1972 Hornets belonged to Wilbert. He learned the game at the feet of coach Dempsey and by sharing the backfield in 1971 with senior sensation Elliott Williams. As a teenage athlete, Wilbert recognized the importance of team play and teamwork, understanding that one talented athlete alone could never achieve a championship for a team. That Montgomery never complained or grew frustrated about playing in Williams's shadow attests to his humility and perseverance, virtues that would be central to his success at the collegiate and professional levels.

More importantly, the "Montgomery Express" did more than slice through defenses and dismantle opposing offensives. It also assisted in knocking down racial barriers in Greenville, Mississippi. When Wilbert first suited up for Greenville in 1971, racial turmoil lay barely beneath the surface as Mississippians struggled to come to grips with integration. The slightest spark might have touched off a firestorm, particularly on the emotional and always volatile gridiron. But coach Dempsey remembered the impact Wilbert had on the Greenville community. "We didn't do anything right that first year," he confessed. "But the second year we had Wilbert. The football players got together on their own and said they were going to do whatever it takes." The Hornets' success on the gridiron then spilled over into the city of Greenville, according to Dempsey, and "united the whole community. And our football team has helped smooth over our problems ever since."[34] Dempsey recently remembered it as a "difficult time, but a good time to go through."[35]

Since Wilbert Montgomery did not emerge as a premier running back until his senior season, he was not highly recruited out Greenville High. Most colleges, apart from a few all-black schools such as Jackson State College, virtually ignored him. Jackson State officials initially thought that they had secured his services, but white coaches from West Texas had intercepted him and wooed the little-known recruit. Just as he had outwitted and outraced high school defenders, Montgomery would do the same to Jackson State coaches, sparking a lingering controversy.

"I Didn't Want to be a Part-Time Player": Wilbert Montgomery's Escape from Mississippi to West Texas

It's hard to say why I picked Abilene Christian. Maybe it's the atmosphere . . . it's kinda quiet around here.

Wilbert Montgomery (quoted in Denne H. Freeman, "Wilbert Montgomery Featured in AP Story," *Abilene Reporter News*, December 1, 1973)

When somebody talks about West Texas, they talk about football.

Brad Allen (quoted in H. G. Bissinger, *Friday Night Lights: A Town, A Team, and A Dream*, 43)

In the summer of 1973, an athletic and emotional tug-of-war ensnared Wilbert Montgomery between black coaches in the Magnolia State and white coaches in Texas. His bold decision to walk away from the Jackson State College Tigers in Mississippi and play football for the Abilene Christian College Wildcats in the Lone Star State ignited a controversy that lingered for many years. That Montgomery initially signed with Abilene Christian College and only later with Jackson State College reveals his indecisiveness and immaturity as a teenager. More significantly, that coaching staffs from two different states verbally sparred over the African American teenager from the Mississippi Delta attests that he was an unusually gifted athlete. In spite of the conflict, Montgomery recently called his choice to play for the Wildcats "the smartest move I ever made."[1]

Varying accounts circulated as to why Wilbert Montgomery abruptly left Jackson State College and enrolled at Abilene Christian College. Because he practiced with the Tigers for four days, Jackson State coaches presumed that Montgomery was satisfied, but they failed to understand their young recruit. "It just makes me sick," lamented Bob Hill, head coach for the Jackson State Tigers. The bewildered coach added, "I walked around all summer long with a smile on my face thinking about Montgomery and (Walter) Payton in the same backfield. I can't understand why he did it. He [Montgomery] was working hard here and seemed happy but I guess they (Abilene) just got to him. Montgomery is a quiet kid and I guess he just believed what they told him."[2]

Sports journalist Jeff Pearlman has recently pointed out that Hill had actually planned to start Walter Payton and Wilbert Montgomery in the same backfield at Jackson State. Recruiting collegiate athletes in the early 1970s was, in the words of coach Hill, "dog-eat-dog," and "Abilene ate my dog."[3] Hill was especially devastated at the end of the 1973 season on learning that Montgomery had rushed for thirty-one touchdowns, and helped lead the Abilene Christian College Wildcats to a National Athletic Intercollegiate Association (NAIA) Championship. Hill could only imagine the success the Jackson State College Tigers would have enjoyed with a Montgomery-Payton tandem.

While Montgomery practiced football on the Jackson State campus, coach Hill knew that his prized recruit received several telephone calls. "But we didn't know it was from Abilene," explained Hill. "We thought it was his girlfriend calling him." Ponto Downing, a sports writer for Jackson's *Clarion-Ledger*, commented that Montgomery went home one weekend to "see a girlfriend" and that was "long enough for Abilene to make the heist." Despite Montgomery's sudden and surprising departure for West Texas, Hill held out "hopes" that he would return to Jackson State College since Charles Brady, a defensive tackle for the Tigers and first cousin of Montgomery's, played there. Brady promised Hill that he would recapture Montgomery and "get him back if it's the last thing he does."[4]

Bob Hill correctly perceived Montgomery's shyness, but he badly misunderstood his competitive spirit. Charles Brady similarly underestimated the grasp Abilene Christian College had on his first cousin as well as Montgomery's delight in and his devotion to the Wildcats. After the 1973 championship campaign, Montgomery averred, "I like ACC and the students here. They treat each other like brothers and sisters. I think I've found my place here." So committed was Montgomery to Abilene Christian College's program that he vowed to quit playing football if he failed to return to the West Texas college after Christmas break. "If I don't come back to ACC, I'll drop out of school and not play football anywhere."[5]

Wilbert Montgomery underscored his appreciation for Abilene Christian College by his willingness to convince other black athletes from his hometown to attend his new school in West Texas. By 1975 six other African American athletes from the Mississippi Delta had signed on with the Wildcats. His brother Cleotha—along with Johnny Sellers, Glenn Washington, Ron McMullin, and twin brothers Hubert and Herbert Curry—joined Wilbert in Texas as student-athletes. Even though Wilbert and his six cohorts insisted that Mississippi had better athletic teams than Texas, they readily acknowledged that there seemed to be less racism in the Lone Star State. Herbert Curry remarked that as a black person in Greenville, Mississippi, "You can be riding along in a car and somebody will pull up beside you, roll down your window and holler, 'Hey, nigger, what you think you're doing anyway.'" Wilbert successfully convinced his younger brother and their friends that the Abilene Christian College community treated people respectfully and impartially. "I just told them what I thought about the school. I told them about the people, how they made you feel. Everybody treats everybody like a sister or brother here. It ain't no big school or nothin' but it teaches the Word—you know it's supposed to be a Christian school."[6] The warmth, friendliness, and acceptance Wilbert found in West Texas differed radically from the hostility he faced in Greenville and the suspicion and distrust he encountered in Jackson. To be sure, Montgomery was not seeking to "get religion"; he yearned for an opportunity to shine on the gridiron.

Wilbert Montgomery's influence back home extended beyond the gridiron, however. He persuaded Odis Dolton, a 6'6" basketball player for the Greenville Hornets, to enroll at Abilene Christian College. Dolton, having promised his dying father that he would complete his studies beyond high school, was determined to attend college. Recruited by the predominantly black Tennessee State College and Jackson State College and by the mostly white University of Mississippi, Dolton rejected their offers because "so much partying [was] going on." He initially signed to play basketball at Treasure Valley Community College in Ontario, Oregon, but Montgomery urged Dolton to visit Abilene Christian. After his initial encounter with the people of West Texas, Dolton "felt very comfortable" because there was "no partying and women" at the athletes' disposal. After having a successful basketball career at Abilene Christian, Dolton earned a bachelor's degree there in 1980 before going on to complete a master's degree from Our Lady of the Lake University in San Antonio. Unlike many African American athletes, Dolton chose to remain in Abilene, where he currently works as the city's Assistant Director of Finance; he even relocated his mother, brothers, and sisters there.[7]

Randy Scott, a 6'8" African American basketball player from Dallas, had a similar experience. During his senior year in high school, Scott received fifty-one scholarship offers before signing with Southern Methodist University (SMU). Coaches from ACC, however, visited Scott's home and seemed to be "honest." Head coach Willard Tate told Scott, "Our program is bigger than basketball." Tate's integrity impressed Scott, who became a Wildcat in 1974. After enrolling at ACC, Scott regretted his decision because of the religious bigotry he encountered. "If you weren't a member of the Church of Christ," Scott recalled, "you got worked over pretty good." He also remembered feeling the sting of racism when he and other black basketball players were thrown out of a white restaurant in Nacogdoches, Texas. At the end of his collegiate career at ACC Scott aspired to play professional basketball, until a terrible car wreck almost tore off his right leg. Scott's medical expenses totaled more than $260,000, but generous white Christians in Abilene and beyond came to his rescue and "paid off all my hospital bills." Like Odis Dolton, Scott graduated from ACU in 1976, and he and his wife, Ruth, have settled in the Abilene area. Scott presently works at ACU, advising the university's Educational Talent Search Program.[8]

Notwithstanding Abilene Christian College's cordiality and caring spirit, several other factors contributed to Wilbert Montgomery's unpopular decision to abandon the Jackson State Tigers. Realizing that Walter Payton was the Tigers' featured running back, Montgomery knew that his playing time would be severely limited. In the winter of 1979 Bill Hart, a sports editor for the *Abilene Reporter News*, asked the former Abilene Christian standout and then all-pro running back for the Philadelphia

Eagles whether he regretted not staying with the Jackson State Tigers and playing with Payton. Montgomery gave an emphatic "No," adding, "I just thought I wouldn't get much playing time the first year there, that's why I left. . . . I don't feel bad about leaving there because I came here and had a good season and career."[9]

Montgomery's teammates at Jackson State attributed Wilbert's departure to his lack of toughness and his inability to compete on the same level as Walter Payton. Matthew Norman, a Tiger defensive back, criticized Montgomery: "He passed out on the field one day from the heat. He just couldn't handle it." Jackson State offensive lineman Jackie Slater recalled that when Montgomery went through the drills, he asked out loud, "Do I really want to go through this?" The Tigers' quarterback Ricky Taylor stated more bluntly, "He snuck out because he couldn't take it. But the guy couldn't carry Walter's water. I don't care what anyone said."[10]

In 1996, when he earned induction into the College Football Hall of Fame, Wilbert Montgomery offered more clarity and displayed more temerity about his decision to exit Jackson State College. He felt that Tigers coaches had been disingenuous with him. "I thought I was lied to," Montgomery explained, "just to get me to sign on the dotted line. At that time I was really torn. I had never sat on the bench my entire life. I was going to end up playing behind Walter Payton." Montgomery sensed that Jackson State coaches plotted to move him to defensive back, since Ricky Young, another outstanding running back from Greenville, was likely Payton's backup.[11]

Jackson State coaches, suspecting that Montgomery might abscond to another college, had assigned players to watch his every move. "While I was there they had these guys," Montgomery remarked, "following me around to make sure I didn't decide to cut out." Disturbed that he was being stalked by "body guards," he decided to catch a ride home with a relative, hiding "in the floor of the car." Montgomery, rehashing his experience at Jackson State twenty-one years later, resented feeling "like I was under guard" and "like I had committed a crime." He admitted his indecisiveness, but explained, "As a kid, I didn't know how to say no to nobody." Envisioning that he would get limited playing time, Montgomery left Jackson State and returned to Greenville, where Abilene Christian recruiters awaited him. Upon learning that Montgomery might not return to Jackson State, four Tigers coaches sped to Greenville, went to his home, and "walked through the front door without knocking." Montgomery, however, ran away to his grandfather's house to avoid confronting the "Jackson Four." One of the big four was probably assistant coach Sylvester Collins, who was instructed "to babysit" Montgomery. "Don't let him out of your sight," stated Hill. "Wherever you go, he goes. Wherever he goes, you go."[12] In spite of Hill's stern instructions, Montgomery still escaped from the Magnolia State.

Several people emboldened Wilbert Montgomery to make the move to West Texas. First, Montgomery's grandfather Andrew Williams, seeing his grandson's fear and reticence, advised him, "[I]f I told them [Jackson State College coaches] what my plans were, they would leave me alone." Second, Cleotha Montgomery, Wilbert's brother, was perhaps the most significant person behind his decision to play football at Abilene Christian. "The biggest thing was my brother, Cleotha," Wilbert testified. "We were both standing there in the bedroom crying. We had been so close. When he gave me that vote of confidence he would follow me to Abilene, that helped my decision."[13] With a Ruth-like loyalty, Cleo kept his promise and enrolled at Abilene Christian College in 1974; both brothers excelled as athletes at the West Texas school and beyond.

Third, various white men collaborated and helped steer Wilbert Montgomery to Abilene Christian College. Jimmy Vickers, a Mississippi native and ACC coach Wally Bullington's cousin, informed the Wildcats coach, "I've seen the best looking running back I've ever seen come through Greenville, Mississippi." Bullington, having heard that sort of comment several times, was not convinced until Vickers and Gary Dempsey, Montgomery's football coach at Greenville High School, graciously shared more film of his star athlete with Bullington.[14] Don Smith, Bullington's assistant at Abilene Christian College, traveled frequently to the Magnolia State to fend off rival gridiron suitors and to sway Montgomery to enroll at the Texas school. After Montgomery initially signed with Abilene Christian College and later with Jackson State College, Smith worked diligently "to re-sell him on ACU all over again." Reflecting on the recruiting battle twenty-six years later, Smith said, "I guess what I did was legal then, but I flew down to Greenville on one of our ex's planes and flew Wilbert back to school (in August)."[15]

Coach Bullington credited Smith with swaying Montgomery to choose the Wildcats over the Tigers, maintaining that "Don [Smith] had a real good influence on Wilbert. He's just a real fine recruiter."[16] But Bullington deserves an equal amount of credit for landing the Mississippi phenom.

When Jackson State coaches accused the West Texas school of stealing Montgomery from them and threatened legal action, Bullington firmly stood his ground. "We had signed Wilbert at Christmas," affirmed Bullington, "and they broke the rules by signing him that spring." Abilene Christian's head coach warned Jackson State officials that "if they called again, he would call the NCAA. That was the last we heard about it."[17] Montgomery himself praised Bullington and the Abilene Christian College community for his matriculation there. "The people there at Abilene Christian University looked at you not as an athlete, but as a person." He further acknowledged Bullington as a "great coach, motivator and teacher."[18]

If Jimmy Vickers, Don Smith, and Wally Bullington collaborated effectively to lure Wilbert Montgomery to Abilene Christian College, Dick and Addie Felts were largely responsible for keeping him there. Dick, a native of San Saba, Texas, and a Abilene Christian football player from 1949 to 1953, managed the school's cafeteria during Wilbert's tenure. His love of strangers, especially black people, "rubbed off on" his wife Addie, a San Antonio native and also an Abilene Christian graduate. Mrs. Felts remembered Montgomery as a "terribly shy" young man, who constantly "looked down when giving answers." Montgomery explained to Addie his diffident demeanor by pointing out that "In Mississippi, we're not allowed to look into the eyes of white women." In this regard, Montgomery was similar to Elvin Hayes, a prominent basketball player from Rayfield, Louisiana, who starred for the Houston Cougars in the mid 1960s. Historian Katherine Lopez has observed that Hayes brought "a lot of baggage" with him from Louisiana to Texas.[19]

Born and reared sixty-three miles from Money, Mississippi, where the brutal murder of Emmett Till occurred, Montgomery and other black Mississippians knew fully the importance of what playwright Richard Wright called the "Ethics of Living Jim Crow."[20] Till, a fourteen-year-old black youth from Chicago, Illinois, visiting his great-uncle Mose Wright in Money, Mississippi, violated the South's most sacred code by saying, "How about a date, baby?" to a twenty-one-year-old white woman, Carolyn Bryant. Roy Bryant, Carolyn's husband, and J. W. Milam abducted Till, beat him, shot him in the head, and dumped his body in the Tallahatchie River.[21] When Montgomery arrived on the Abilene Christian campus, he bore this disturbing story deep within his soul and it doubtlessly affected how he interacted with white women such as Addie Felts.

Despite, or perhaps because of, the racial and social baggage he brought with him from the Mississippi Delta, Wilbert Montgomery's relationship with the Felts family proved a major turning point in his transition to life in the Lone Star State. The Feltses relieved his homesickness, obliterated misgivings he had about white people in West Texas, and helped him embrace the mostly white Abilene Christian community; in return he endeared himself to the West Texas school. One September afternoon in 1973, Dick Felts invited Montgomery to his home; by December, the Felts had adopted the black student-athlete into their family.[22] Before he returned to his Mississippi home for the Christmas holidays, Montgomery openly acknowledged that the Felts had become his surrogate parents, stating, "I call them my second father and second mother. I love their kids like I would my own brothers and sisters."[23] Abilene Christian coaches, in the wake of threats from Jackson State College officials, feared that their star running back would not return to Abilene, so the Feltses drove to Mississippi, picked up Montgomery, and brought him back to Abilene for the duration of the holiday season.[24]

Of all the white residents in Abilene, Texas, the Felts family proved most pivotal in smoothing Wilbert Montgomery's transition from the Magnolia State to West Texas. The Feltses, devout members of the Hamby Church of Christ, often took him to worship with them. Montgomery, while attending a gospel meeting in Hawley, Texas, conducted by black evangelist John C. Whitley, received baptism into the Church of Christ. After learning that Montgomery had never been given a birthday party, the Feltses planned to celebrate the special occasion at their home, but he never showed up because, in Addie Felts's words, "It scared him." When Montgomery accidentally shot a hole in their ceiling with Dick's shotgun, the Feltses shrugged off the incident as they would have with one of their own boys. Mr. Felts then taught Montgomery how to handle guns properly and often took the student-athlete on hunting excursions.[25]

In addition to the Felts family, John C. Whitley, ACC's first African American faculty member, helped Montgomery transition into a rigorous academic environment. A native of Fort Smith, Arkansas, and a graduate of Southwestern Christian College and Pepperdine University, Whitley began teaching at ACC in 1970. Observing that Montgomery was athletically gifted, but "deficient academically," Whitley intervened with ACC faculty members and convinced them to give the Mississippi athlete oral exams rather written exams, since he had difficulty writing and reading with comprehension. Whitley recently acknowledged that Montgomery used his "natural ability" to "break down" racist attitudes held by some of ACC's coaching staff, players, and students in general. Indeed, Whitley further recalled that racism was "prominent" on ACC's campus, even on the gridiron. The coaching staff, according to Whitley, relied on black players to advance the ball downfield, but pulled them out near the goal line. Wilbert Montgomery sometimes prevented this from happening by returning a kickoff back for a score. There was "no stopping that boy," stressed Whitley.[26]

In essence, Wilbert Montgomery was not a student-athlete; he was an "athlete-student." Unlike Paul Robeson, who excelled at Rutgers University as a "scholar-athlete," Montgomery was in many ways the direct opposite. Robeson benefited from a two-parent family who instilled in him the "virtues of hard work and the attainment of knowledge." Montgomery received an abiding work ethic from his mother and grandparents, but the emphasis on academic achievement was missing. Robeson was a "scholar-baller," that is, he possessed both "academic and athletic prowess." This was not true of Montgomery. David Merrell, a longtime English professor at ACC, has pointed out that Montgomery was unsure whether he "could be a student at ACC or not." The Mississippi native was weak academically, but not athletically. Wilbert, added Merrell, was "shy, but not in athletic venues. He could stand flat-footed and dunk a basketball. He had muscle. He was an athlete!" Unlike Robeson, who used his athletic prowess at Rutgers University to study at Columbia Law School, Montgomery appeared to enter ACC with his heart set on becoming the next Gale Sayers.[27]

Even though Wilbert Montgomery never conformed to the image of Paul Robeson, he never forgot his warm reception from the ACC community. ACC's student body embraced Montgomery because of his exploits on the football field. A few days before ACC's 1973 championship game against Elon University, the *Abilene Reporter News* published a photograph of Montgomery standing between two white female students, insinuating that there was no prohibition against a black athlete mingling freely with white girls. A winning season seemingly helped melt away some of the aversion whites harbored against the binary of white females and black males. Yet Randy Scott, Wilbert's classmate, recently noted that even though there was no official ban on interracial dating at ACC, there was a covert, unwritten policy and "you knew it was there."[28]

Even though the mixing of white females with black males kindled the ire of some whites in Abilene, most of the ACC community embraced Montgomery as a player and person. He especially loved the Felts family, and they, in turn, genuinely loved him. When he was inducted into the College Football Hall of Fame in 1996, Montgomery expressed his own fondness for the Abilene Christian University community. "The people there at Abilene Christian University looked at you not as an athlete, but as a person." He added, "In Abilene, the people are so genuine. If people told you something, you'd take them at their word. I look at it as if Abilene is my family."[29] When Montgomery spoke those words, he had in mind Abilene Christian's coaches—Wally Bullington, Don Smith, and Ted Sitton, among others—his teammates, and fellow classmates; but he especially intended those remarks for Dick and Addie Felts. More significantly, Montgomery learned to trust the white coaches in west Texas because of his positive experiences with Gary Dempsey in the Magnolia State.

Wilbert Montgomery chose to leave Jackson State College and enroll at Abilene Christian College because he wanted to play as a freshman. Jimmie Giles, a high school classmate of Wilbert's at Greenville High, remembered his impatience: "He had to wait his turn. He wasn't going to move Payton out."[30] But Montgomery believed that he was as good, if not better, than any other running back, including Walter Payton. "To play as a freshman, I had to leave," he insisted. "I didn't want to be a part-time player."[31] Montgomery was a shy young man, but he possessed a fierce competitive spirit. And he wanted to be free, free to showcase his special talent on the collegiate level as a freshman, free from restrictions that African American coaches at Jackson State College intended to impose on him as a "part-time player," and—especially—free from the racial hatred that permeated his home state. Therein lies the paradox: Wilbert Montgomery, a black teenager from the Mississippi Delta, would not be allowed to shine on his own terms as a running back at a predominantly black school in his home state. In order to do that, he had to seek greener—or whiter—pastures in West Texas.

Part II

Wilbert Montgomery and the
West Texas Experience, 1973–1976

"We're Gonna' Surprise Lots of Folks": Wilbert Montgomery, the Abilene Christian Wildcats, and the 1973 Championship Season

He [Wilbert Montgomery] has an unreal combination of all the running skills—speed, quickness, moves and he's strong enough in the thighs to break tackles. He broke six tackles on one run. On another four Southwest Texas players had him boxed in and he burst right through them.

Garner Roberts, ACC Sports Information Director (quoted in Denne H. Freeman, "Wilbert Montgomery Featured in AP Story," *Abilene Reporter News*, December 1, 1973)

[Gale] Sayers was a fantastic runner.... I want to be just like him.

Wilbert Montgomery (quoted in Freeman, "Wilbert Montgomery Featured in AP Story")

The Abilene Christian College Wildcats finished their 1972 season with a dismal record of three wins and eight losses. Optimism and enthusiasm, however, lifted the 1973 squad as they prepared for a new season. The return of twenty-seven lettermen—including nine defensive and seven offensive starters—presented the Wildcats with what coach Wally Bullington called his "best team in three years at ACC."[1] Allen Wilson, an African American defensive back from Midland, Texas, exuded even more confidence, exclaiming, "Man, we're gonna' have a good ballclub, you just wait and see. I think we're gonna' surprise lots of folks. I just hope the other schools take us lightly 'cuz we're gonna' sneak up on 'em."[2] A diligent coaching staff joined with players on both offense and defense lent currency to "Snowball," Wilson's prophecy. The Wildcats won the 1973 National Athletic Intercollegiate Association (NAIA) Championship largely because of their "big surprise" from the Mississippi Delta, Wilbert Montgomery.

ACC owed their 1973 Lone Star Conference (LSC) title as well as their NAIA championship to several factors. First, all great teams must have great coaching, and ACC's head coach and athletic director, Wally Bullington, was accustomed to winning ways. Bullington attended ACC from 1949 to 1953; in 1950 he played on the only undefeated squad in Wildcat history. Upon graduation, Bullington assisted the renowned Chuck Moser, the Abilene High Eagles' head coach, who led his "Warbirds" to a Texas state record of forty-nine consecutive victories from 1954 to 1957. When Bullington took the reins of ACC's gridiron program in 1969, he set out to transform the Wildcats into contenders. After visiting coaching staffs at the University of Houston, Florida State University, and the Dallas Cowboys, Bullington switched from the wishbone offense and in 1973 installed the pro-passing game at ACC. Hubert Pickett, ACC's running back, recalled Wally Bullington as more than a meticulous coach; he was "a loving Christian" who "loved you [as a player] and looked out for you." Defensive back Bob Strader added that ACC's head coach "used his profession to teach young men about Jesus." He was a "great motivator." Ove Johansson, ACC's kicker during the 1976 season, acknowledged that Bullington had an "incredible impact on [his] life." He constantly "built up" his players. "I wanted to kick for him. I wanted to perform for him," Johansson testified.[3]

In order to execute his new pro-passing offense, Bullington knew that he had to groom his veteran quarterback, Clint Longley. A 6'1" junior from Littleton, Colorado, Longley, nicknamed the "Purple Vindicator" by ACC students, had amassed just 2,062 passing yards and nine touchdowns during the 1972 season.[4] But the following year he engineered 3,167 passing yards and twenty-eight touchdowns in Bullington's new offensive scheme.[5] Longley threw primarily to Richard Williams and Greg Stirman.

A speedy senior receiver from Gainesville, Florida, Williams began the 1973 season on the bench because he dropped too many passes, as coach Bullington commented that Williams had "always run beautiful patterns, but his consistency has hurt him."[6] The ACC coaching staff named David Henson, a transfer from Blinn Junior College, as starting receiver for the season opener against Arkansas State University (ASU), but after coming off the bench and catching Longley touchdown passes of 90, 10, and 40 yards, Williams regained his starting position and never relinquished it.[7] By season's end Williams's performance had earned him a spot on the 1973 LSC All-Conference Team.[8]

Greg Stirman's roots ran deep in the ACC community. His father, Fred Stirman, played football for the Wildcats in the late 1940s. After a successful stint at Abilene High School, 6'4" son Greg enrolled at ACC, where he starred at the tight end position. The *Optimist*, ACC's student newspaper, named Greg Player of the Week after he hauled in six passes for 90 yards against Sul Ross. "I don't know if there is a better tight end in the southwest," commended coach Bullington. "He's a good one, blocking and catching passes, especially on important third down plays. He's so consistent, the more pressure, the better he plays."[9] With the Wildcats' success meshing with his own efficiency, Greg Stirman also won a place on the 1973 LSC All-Conference Team.[10]

Yet without a stout offensive line, Clint Longley's passing production would have been reduced. Before the start of the 1973 campaign, Bullington admitted that ACC's offensive line "lacks depth."[11] He added, "This is a big question mark right now. We've got some young kids in there and some guys that don't have much experience. They've got to come on and really mature if we're going to move the ball." He also worried about the Wildcats' ability to score when the offense moved into the red zone.[12] Anchored by left tackle Garry Moore, left guard Bryan Smith, center Clint Owens, right guard Mike Layfield, and right tackle Don Harrison, the ACC offensive line improved steadily through the course of the season, erasing their coach's doubts. Wilbert Montgomery, after being named to the "Little All-America" team at the end of the 1973 season, bestowed perhaps the highest compliment upon his blockers when he declared, "I couldn't have made it if it wasn't for the front line."[13] Montgomery understood that his productivity in the backfield, as well as the success of the entire Wildcat offense, rested on the performance and proficiency of the guys up front.

After they gave up fifty-six points and more than 500 yards in their opening loss, sports writer Mark McDonald, covering college football for the *Abilene Reporter News*, dubbed the 1973 ACC defense the "invisible men."[14] Knowing that his defenders would be outsized by LSC foes, K. Y. Owens, the Wildcats' defensive coordinator, determined to exploit his players' speed and quickness. Leroy Polnick, a 5'11" product from Cooper High in Abilene, had played quarterback in high school, but ACC coaches moved him first to safety and then to linebacker. Weighing in at 195 pounds and running a 4.8 in the 40-yard dash, Polnick certainly was not the biggest (or fastest) linebacker in the LSC, but he offered a "dependable hand" during the 1973 campaign with his "steady play."[15]

ACC's coaching staff moved Ken Laminack from weak safety "back home" to linebacker to cover receivers coming out of the backfield. Realizing the importance of his new position, Laminack explained that "Anything outside is extra yardage or a touchdown if I don't make the play."[16] Another anchor of ACC's defense was Charles "Cheesee" Hinson, a transfer from Blinn Junior College. Hinson—a diminutive 5'8.5", 180-pound linebacker—confessed, "I like a team that tries to get wide on us better than a team with a lot of brute force. My main asset is quickness and speed, so I like to move around quite a bit."[17] After their initial loss to Arkansas State, the Wildcats' "invisible men" virtually manhandled their remaining opponents, even racking up two shutouts: 29–0 against Sul Ross and 27–0 against Angelo State. Coach Owens quickly put a positive spin on the label "invisible men," observing, "You can't block a guy you can't see, you know"[18], and Mark McDonald wrote after ACC smashed Southwest Texas State University, 41–7, that "Linebacker Cheesee Hinson keyed the invisible men in a defensive performance that has taken an abrupt about-face since the Wildcats dropped a 56–46 decision to Arkansas State."[19]

Coach Wally Bullington's fresh and pass-happy offense quickly increased the attendance at Wildcat home games. Some contests at Shotwell Stadium in Abilene in 1973 boasted crowds of more than ten thousand, well over a tenth of the city's population. The ACC student body, just over three thousand strong, not only helped pack Shotwell Stadium for home games but also accompanied the team on away games; as Mark McDonald noted, "No football team in the Lone Star Conference can boast the student support received by the Abilene Christian Wildcats this fall".[20] The 180-piece Big Purple Band often paid their own way to cheer on their Wildcats, and each Thursday at noon Bullington gave a pep talk to the band, thanking and encouraging them. Greg Stirman, ACC's standout tight end, often led the band in the school's song after every win.

Bullington understood that freshman running back Wilbert Montgomery was, of course, a major "drawing card."[21] Bolstered by a smart and seasoned coaching staff, a sharp-shooting quarterback, a bulldozing offensive line, the "invisible men" on defense, and a boisterous fan base, the ACC Wildcats surprised all of their gridiron opponents in 1973. The biggest surprise for the Wildcats, however, was Montgomery, the dazzling back from the Mississippi Delta, who gave ACC's offense "a breakaway threat that they have lacked in the past."[22] After Montgomery ran a 4.5 in the 40-yard dash during two-a-day practices, coach Bullington had raved: "Ooooo! Can he scoot, and he's got good hands."[23] A few weeks later during a scrimmage against the crosstown rivals, the McMurry Indians, Montgomery foreshadowed his gridiron gifts with impressive moves, demonstrating "all the equipment" of a "superstar."[24]

When Wilbert Montgomery enrolled at ACC in the fall of 1973, he was one of 3,190 students.[25] The first African American students, Larry Bonner, Billy Curl, and Washington D. Harris, matriculated at ACC in 1961; seven years later the first black athlete at ACC, Henry Willis, played basketball for the Wildcats. A few years later the Christian school attracted two black professors, John C. Whitley and Billy Van Jones. Whitley, the first black faculty member at ACC, taught Bible from 1970 to 1974; Jones, a PhD candidate at the University of Houston, served first as a visiting professor in 1973.[26] Like much of the rest of the country in the late 1960s and early 1970s, Abilene was a racially divided city still coping with the turbulent events of the civil rights era. African Americans in Abilene had established Woodson High School in the early 1940s to educate their children, yet in comparison to their counterparts for whites, blacks' facilities were often second-rate. One disgruntled black parent testified that their children consistently received "leftovers . . . leftover books, leftover desks, leftover football uniforms, leftover band uniforms" from the more affluent white schools. When African American students began attending all-white schools in 1962, white residents strongly resented their presence. L. L. Schults, a concerned white parent, acknowledged, "I have 4 children all going to school but one and they are not going to school with the Negroes!!" In Schults's view and in the opinion of many other white Texans, African Americans were essentially "outsiders."[27]

Racist perspectives that existed in the Abilene community also per-

Wilbert Montgomery (28) on the move for the ACC Wildcats, ca. 1973.
Courtesy of Abilene Christian University.

vaded the ACC campus. To help address lingering racial issues, Abilene city officials established the Human Relations Committee, while ACC administrators invited Arthur L. Smith (now Molefi Kete Asante), director of the Center for Afro-American Studies at the University of California at Los Angeles to assist the ACC community "in developing a better understanding in communications principles as applied to interracial dialogue."[28] Despite the push for a more integrated campus, some ACC students asserted that a "growing rage" pervaded the college because of the mistreatment of black students and because "blacks and whites at ACC" failed to communicate.[29]

The athletic prowess of Wilbert Montgomery played a significant role in improving race relations at ACC and the Abilene community. Addie Felts, Montgomery's surrogate mother and an ACC physical education instructor, has insisted that the Mississippi Delta native "definitely" helped improve race relations at the West Texas campus. He was "accepted because he was a fantastic football player" and "such a star." His enrollment at ACC marked the "beginning a whole new era" because he attracted so much media attention to the school, beginning with the 1973 season, and because he swayed other black student-athletes from his hometown to join him at his West Texas school.[30] Hubert Pickett, who considered it an "honor to throw blocks for" Wilbert Montgomery, maintained that he "helped to bridge cultural gaps in Abilene and West Texas" because "people came from all around to see us play."[31]

Like Jackie Robinson, Willie Mays, Marcus Dupree, and other African American athletes in predominantly white settings, Wilbert Montgomery helped change many West Texans' perceptions of black people. Even though the Wildcats had lost their season opener to Arkansas State, ACC displayed promising signs. Quarterback Clint Longley threw a record six touchdown passes, and Montgomery caught a short pass and scampered 39 yards for his first collegiate touchdown in that contest. Head coach Wally Bullington commented to offensive coordinator Ted Sitton after Montgomery's first score, "I think we have an outstanding back."[32] The *Abilene Reporter News* explained, "It was the first time Montgomery touched the football in his young collegiate career and gave a hint of his glistening potential."[33]

For the remainder of the 1973 season, Montgomery consistently displayed his natural skill by dashing past and slipping around opposing defenders. In their second game, the LSC opener against Texas A&I, the Wildcats trounced their opponents 35–14. Hubert Pickett rushed for 139 yards in spite of a broken nose; Montgomery dazzled the crowd with a 39-yard touchdown run, finishing the game with 77 rushing yards, 9 receiving yards, and two touchdowns. Mark McDonald reported, "The opening play of the fourth quarter saw Montgomery, an elusive freshman blessed with raw running instincts, stun the Javelina defense with a 39-yard scamper. Montgomery's quick feet enabled him to sweep the A&I left flank, reverse his field, cut back to the sidelines and leave several exasperated Hogs in his wake."[34]

Reporter Bill Hart also commented that Wilbert Montgomery's fancy footwork fired the ACC crowd, as "time after time he brought the crowd to their feet with his fancy-dan running, changing speed and direction without breaking stride."[35] When asked about his wraith-like style, Montgomery cast back to his boyhood: "I used to put tires in the street and try to run through them without breaking stride."[36] Even though Hubert Pickett broke his nose during this game, he vowed to play in the next contest: "I can't afford to sit out the way Montgomery is pushing me." Pickett spoke fondly of their friendly competition, explaining that "He pushes me and I push him, and competition makes us both better."[37] And in the games ahead opponents keyed on Montgomery at their own peril since Pickett ran so effectively.

In ACC's third game against the Southwest Texas State Bobcats, quarterback Clint Longley passed for 444 yards and four scores, connecting with Montgomery for 119 yards and all of the touchdowns. "It boggles one's mind," wrote Mark McDonald, "to imagine this 185 pound tailback playing in high school only one year ago."[38] After Montgomery's 50-yard touchdown dash against the Bobcats, the *Optimist* reported that "the ACC bench rushed to meet him offering their congratulations."[39] More than a sure-handed pass catcher out of the backfield, Montgomery, in only his fourth game as a Wildcat, ripped through the Stephen F. Austin Lumberjacks' defense for 146 yards, scored six touchdowns, and led his team to an extraordinary 57–50 victory.[40] After this impressive performance against the Lumberjacks, Montgomery garnered national attention when *Sports Illustrated* featured him as the NAIA leading scorer.[41] In his fifth game, Montgomery tallied just 53 yards and one touchdown, as an ankle injury sidelined him in the Wildcats' sixth game against Sul Ross. Despite Montgomery's absence, ACC blanked Sul Ross, 29–0.[42]

After taking a handoff from quarterback Clint Longley (19), Wilbert Montgomery (28) dashes toward the line of scrimmage behind the solid blocking of fullback Hubert Pickett (42), 1973. Courtesy of Abilene Christian University.

In game seven Montgomery returned to the field with full force, rushing for 165 yards on twenty-two carries, tallying three touchdowns against the Angelo State University Rams.[43] Picking up still more steam, Montgomery darted past Tarleton State defenders for 168 yards on the ground, 35 receiving yards, and four more touchdowns.[44] Against Sam Houston State, in ACC's ninth game, Montgomery sliced through Bearkat defenders for five more scores—four on the ground (sixteen carries and 109 yards) and one receiving (two catches and 49 yards).[45] Montgomery and the ACC Wildcats ended the regular season against Howard Payne before a capacity crowd of fifteen thousand at Shotwell Stadium. The freshman from Mississippi carried twenty-six times for 127 yards and three touchdowns; he added three catches for 65 yards and one more touchdown. Montgomery wrapped up the regular season with a record-breaking thirty-one touchdowns and a new point mark, eclipsing the standard set by O. J. Simpson of the University of Southern California and Billy Clyde Puckett of Slippery Rock University.[46] By season's end, the Wildcats boasted a 9–1 record and the nation's leading scorer as Montgomery piled up 1,265 total yards (854 rushing yards and 411 receiving yards).[47] The previous year ACC's offense had rushed for a total of 1,021 yards[48]; Montgomery's offensive output alone exceeded the previous year's team efforts. Coach Wally Bullington's new pro-passing offense and his outstanding running back from the Magnolia State had turned the corner for the Wildcat football program.

Because of Wilbert Montgomery's feats on the gridiron, he and his ACC Wildcats attracted national attention. Even though he was merely a freshman, professional scouts drooled over Montgomery, and major colleges across the country that had ignored him during high school years now cast "longing glances." "If somebody does get him away from us," Wally Bullington sternly warned, "the investigation what's going to follow will make Watergate look small." ACC sports information director Garner Roberts observed, "Scouts come to see (quarterback) Clint Longley and (receiver) Rich Williams and Wilbert knocks their eyes out." Reed Johnson, scout for the Dallas Cowboys, told Roberts that "All three of those boys could play for any team in the Big Eight or the Southwest Conference. Montgomery is something else."[49] The young Mississippian, however, spurned the attention, complaining, "I don't like all this publicity . . . can't go down the street without people recognizing me. . . . [I]t's all a little confusing."[50]

While the local and national media raved about Montgomery's exploits, he and his Wildcat teammates focused on the postseason and their next foe, the Langston University Lions, an all-black team from Oklahoma that boasted a ferocious defense featuring Thomas "Hollywood" Henderson, future linebacker for the Dallas Cowboys. Henderson and his "dirty" crew warned Montgomery that they would "take [him] out and [he] wouldn't be around at the finish." The threats, Montgomery confessed, only made "[him] play harder."[51] A "fired up" Montgomery carried the ball twenty-four times for 168 yards and four touchdowns in a 34–6 Wildcat victory, slowed not at all by the vaunted Langston defense.

Officials disqualified three Langston players for illegal hits, and the emotions on the field spilled over onto the sidelines and into the stands of the Langston Lions. Lions quarterback Prinson Poindexter complained, "We've had to play with poor officiating before and were expecting it. I'm not using the officiating as an excuse—we've played against worse and won."[52] Langston fans protested that they were cheated, and Lions cheerleaders railed, "You damn right, we got cheated. This is the Texas Watergate, you fellas," and "You honky rats—We're No. 1."[53] Most players from both teams seemed more cordial, recognizing the strengths in each opposing squad. "They do have a good defense," ACC tight end Greg Stirman testified. "That 91 (Henderson) is probably one of the best football players we've played against." Clint Longley agreed: "I've never played against anyone as good as 91. He's a great football player."[54]

Members of the Langston Lions similarly commended ACC players, especially Wilbert Montgomery and Clint Longley. Defensive end Von Holmes called Montgomery a "good back" and a "pretty nice back" before summarizing, "Montgomery and Longley are tough cookies—especially Longley. I was trying to put him out of the game, but he can take a lick—he's smart too."[55] Thomas Henderson, the Lions' premier defensive player, remarked, "They're the best team we've played this season. But they couldn't go through our conference without losing." Fourteen years later, Henderson remembered both Longley and Montgomery, calling ACC a "real football team": "We were out there to kick the hell out of somebody but they really took it to us."[56] Lions head coach Albert Shoats similarly confessed to mixed emotions. On the one hand, he lauded Montgomery as "one of the best we've faced"; on the other hand, he insisted that ACC could not go through the Oklahoma Collegiate Conference (OCC) unblemished.[57]

Brushing past the opinions of the Langston Lions, ACC Wildcats turned their attention to the national championship game with Elon College, a United Church of Christ school from North Carolina. Knowing that Elon stood undefeated and boasted a well-balanced offensive and defensive squad, coach Wally Bullington prepared his team thoroughly and methodically. On Monday he worked his Wildcats on timing and loosening their "muscles made sore last week." The next day the scout team ran the opponents' plays, and on Wednesday Bullington emphasized and polished the passing game and special team assignments. The LSC champs reviewed their defensive strategy, their short yardage formation, and their two-minute drill during Thursday's practice, before leaving for Shreve-

Wilbert Montgomery slashing through Elon defenders during the 1973 national title game. After amassing 238 all-purpose yards, Montgomery earned MVP honors. Courtesy of Abilene Christian University.

port, Louisiana—site of the title game—on Friday morning. At a local high school field they loosened up "to get some of the bus ride out of us."[58]

Armed with a sound game plan and supported by over four thousand fans, the ACC Wildcats easily vanquished Elon College, 42–14, as Clint Longley passed for 341 yards and Wilbert Montgomery, although bothered by an asthma attack and an upset stomach, splashed through the Fighting Christians' defense for 238 all-purpose yards, earning the Most Valuable Offensive Player award. Mark McDonald summed up ACC's team effort thus: "The running of tailback Wilbert Montgomery, the passing of Clint Longley and the defense of Chip Martin, Jan Brown and Cheesee Hinson made the victory look ridiculously easy." Richard Williams, happy to be

After winning the NAIA national championship in 1973, running back Wilbert Montgomery and quarterback Clint Longley stand beside the championship trophy. Courtesy of Abilene Christian University.

performing before his parents for the first time in during his college career, collected five passes for 119 yards and "one beautiful touchdown." Williams spoke candidly of the contest, saying, "We were expecting them to be a better team. They've been ranked No. 1 most of the season, but I can't figure out why. We should have been ranked No. 1 a long time ago."[59]

Abilene Christian College, after losing the season's first game against Arkansas State, regrouped, defeated each opponent, and won the 1973 national championship. Blessed with an exceptional coaching staff, an all-star quarterback, a quick and passionate defense, and—most importantly—a nineteen-year-old black athlete from the Mississippi Delta, ACC surprised all of their gridiron foes during the 1973 campaign. So impressed were LSC officials that they bestowed Coach of the Year honors on Wally Bullington and All-America first team honors on Clint Longley, Richard Williams, Greg Stirman, Jan Brown, and Wilbert Montgomery.[60] Of these outstanding players, none shone more brightly than the black star from the Mississippi Delta.

Wilbert Montgomery did more than lead the ACC Wildcats to the NAIA national title, however. He also helped alter racial perceptions and eliminate racial barriers at a Christian college in West Texas where some viewed black people as outcasts and outsiders.[61] While Montgomery dazzled fans in West Texas with his amazing talent on the gridiron, whites at ACC simultaneously grew more accepting and more appreciative of black athletes and of black students in general. English professor David Merrell has held that Montgomery's coming to the ACC community proved "very significant." By leading the Wildcats to a national championship as a freshman, he helped move the Christian college from being "tolerant" of African Americans to being "more accepting" of them.[62]

John C. Whitley, a black Bible professor at ACC, remembered attending the national championship game in Shreveport, Louisiana, with Charles Hodge, a white preacher from Texas. Whitley recalled that as Wilbert Montgomery carried the football down the field toward the goal line, Hodge ran in the same direction toward the end zone in the bleachers. Hodge recently observed, "Wilbert not only won ball games . . . he opened the doors for blacks at ACC."[63] Rena Wright, a fellow African American student at ACC during Montgomery's tenure, pointed out that when Wilbert carried the ball, it was the "only time [she] ever saw them [white people] pulling for us." She also recalled seeing junior high and high school students, mostly white, freely interacting with Wilbert and asking him questions.[64] One black Texan, commenting on the impact of African American athlete on race relations, pointed out that many white people in West Texas "suspended all racist judgments when they sat in the stands and gazed down at a football field or a basketball court or a baseball diamond."[65] Thus, during the 1973 football campaign, Montgomery, in addition to breaking records and garnering honors, also won the hearts of the ACC community—a feat more honorable, and far more important—than titles and trophies.

The 1973 ACC National Championship Team. Courtesy of Abilene Christian University. *First row:* Allen Wilson (31), Steve Ricks (72), Richard Lepard (33), Gregg Pritchard (84), Dub Stocker (60), Jan Brown (25), Bob Strader (40), Jimmy Rutland (62), *Second row:* Stewart Powers (89), Donald Callahan (54), Paul Parker (35), Roy Colvin (34), Reggie Hunter (20), Duff Phipps (23), Tommy Smith (76), Jim Reese (14), Charles Hinson (10). *Third row:* Clint Owens (52), John Isom (51), Leroy Polnick (46), Cassy Garza (21), David Haynes (32), Mike Burk (24), Clint Longley (19), Mark Culwell (45), Roger Samoff (56). *Fourth row:* Frank Vallie (70), Ken Laminack (41), Bob Harmon (66), Dan Cobb (30), John Usrey (68), Mark McCurley (50), Tim Botkin (80), Danny King. *Fifth row:* Don Harrison (73), Monty Tuttle (22), Billy Curbo (77), Chuck Lawson (11), Mike Layfield (64), Chip Martin (65), Jay Laminack (83), Sonny Moyers (78). *Sixth row:* Richard Williams (88), Allen Stephens (44), Randall Cobb (75), Raymond Crosier (17), Hubert Pickett (42), Jay Reeves (15), Steve Powers (87). *Seventh row:* Wilbert Montgomery (28), David Henson (81), Toby York (12), Kevin McLeod (82), Greg Stirman (85), Gary Stirman (86), Garry Moore (71), Herman Nelson (79). *Back row:* Dave Wood (manager), Britt Gamble (trainer), Donnie Davidson (trainer), Glen Lawrence (manager), Bruce Billingsley (manager), Fred Cawyer (trainer).

Dynamite on "The Hill": Wilbert Montgomery and the Abilene Christian Wildcats in 1974

First of all, there is no such thing as a "free" ride. A black athlete pays dearly with his blood, sweat, tears, and ultimately with some portion of his manhood, for the questionable right to represent his school on the athletic field.

Harry Edwards, *The Revolt of the Black Athlete*, 16

You're not going to believe this, but being black is the greatest burden I've had to bear.

Arthur Ashe (quoted in Arthur Ashe and Arnold Rampersad, *Days of Grace: A Memoir*, 126)

When opposing coaches and players within and outside of the Lone Star Conference (LSC) faced Wilbert Montgomery for the first time in 1973, most had never encountered an athlete with such a rare combination of blinding quickness, speed, and physical power. Montgomery, however, never again during his collegiate career amassed the yardage and touchdowns he did that year. After 1973, foes knew of his capabilities and prepared more diligently and more thoroughly to defend against him. Beyond this, injuries cut deeply into his playing time. Unlike in 1973, when the smooth-stepping freshman rushed for 854 yards and more than thirty touchdowns, the following year he totaled 657 yards on the ground and scored seventeen touchdowns. "You may have noticed," explained sports writer Art Lawler, "that opposing defenses took the trouble to key on him once in a while—like every down."[1] Defensive coordinators now understood that by slowing ACC's leading ground gainer, they could simultaneously severely curtail the Wildcats' offense.

The pressure to duplicate his 1973 achievements on the field also frustrated Montgomery and sparked confrontations with teammates and classmates off the field. "With defenses keying on him, the pressure on Montgomery began to mount. Then finally," added journalist Mark McDonald, "the normally placid and retiring athlete exploded, striking a team mate during a dormitory flareup. It was a shocking display of frustration that put a walk on student-athlete in the hospital overnight."[2] This incident had occurred in Edwards Hall on the ACC campus where Montgomery lived. When he walked into a room occupied by fellow African American athletes Gary Graham and Johnny Perkins, Montgomery detected a terrible odor and exclaimed, "It smells in this room." Graham sarcastically replied, "It must be your top lip." Montgomery challenged Graham to stand up and say that to his face. Graham stood and repeated his remarks and Montgomery pushed him. Graham then swung at Montgomery, who dodged the blow and came back with a stiff uppercut that knocked Graham out.[3]

The Montgomery-Graham clash points up Montgomery's "shocking display of frustration." Although white sports writers, white coaches, and white spectators admiringly observed his athletic prowess, few, if any, knew of his heated temper and the rage that boiled inside. Although many white fans have expected black athletes to be meek, mild, and submissive, sports sociologist Harry Edwards has looked more deeply, challenging this conventional wisdom. He understood that white Americans, since the days of chattel enslavement, viewed African American men as meek and mild, observing that "Black men, engaged in violent, aggressive, competitive sports actually were regarded as hereditarily non-violent! Moreover, black athletes were expected to be submissive." Consequently, in the 1930s white Americans gladly crowned boxer Joe Louis champion largely because of his meek, mild, and unassuming disposition. Louis, in the view of many whites, was the "antithesis of Jack Johnson," a black champion

Wilbert Montgomery while playing for Abilene Christian University, 1973. Courtesy of Abilene Christian University.

in the early twentieth century who refused to stay in his so-called place. Johnson defied white custom and authority not only by pummeling white competitors in the boxing ring but also by sleeping with white women behind closed doors. Historian Randy Roberts has poignantly noted, "Everything Louis did, every image he projected, carried the same message: 'I am not Jack Johnson.'" In 1964, when Don Chaney, Elvin Hayes, and Warren McVea enrolled at the University of Houston, they certainly understood that the white establishment there expected them to be meek and know their place.[4] Beyond societal generalities, Montgomery's grandfather Andrew Williams was a boxer who taught his grandson how to fight and how to defend himself. Williams trained young Wilbert to "hit it and quit it," that is, knock out a foe with one punch.[5] Montgomery, then, was more than simply a singularly talented athlete; he was a passionate young human being with great pride, and resentful of insults from others—be they black or white.

In spite of Wilbert's cultural baggage from his youth in the Magnolia State, his athletic prowess meant that the ACC Wildcats were fresh off a newly minted NAIA championship; so head coach Wally Bullington headed into the 1974 gridiron season with high expectations. After having signed two more highly touted athletes from the Mississippi Delta, excitement permeated the ACC community. Cleotha Montgomery, an all-star athlete whom the University of Mississippi considered "its bluest of blue chippers," followed his older brother to West Texas. Unlike his brother Wilbert, Cleo was "academically motivated" and an extrovert who freely mingled and interacted with ACC students and faculty members. If Wilbert was a baller-scholar, Cleo became a "scholar-baller." Bob Strader, a former teammate of the Montgomery brothers, recently compared the duo, observing, "Wilbert was the crack in the dam, but Cleo broke open the dam." David Merrell remembered that while Wilbert tended to be "shy, sullen, and withdrawn," it was "hard not to like Cleo." He was so "outgoing" that he "never met a person who didn't like him."[6] Consequently, not only did Wilbert affect race relations at ACC, but his brother was equally influential on campus, if not more so.

After enrolling at ACC, Cleo said, "Last year when Wilbert was confused about where he was going, I told him anywhere he went, I'd go too." Wilbert and Cleo's cousin Ron McMullin also joined the Wildcats. Heavily recruited by almost twenty major universities, including Alabama, Miami, and Notre Dame, McMullin chose to play at ACC. Because of these two

Greenville High School coach Gary Dempsey stands proudly between Cleotha
Montgomery (*left*) and Charles Hall (*right*). Even though both Montgomery and
Hall were highly recruited athletes coming out of Mississippi, they signed with the
ACC Wildcats and followed Wilbert Montgomery to West Texas in 1974. Courtesy of
Abilene Christian University.

signees from Mississippi, sportswriter Bill Hart dubbed Wilbert "the pipe-
line . . . on the Hill."[7]

Despite adding standout recruits from Mississippi and enjoying better "overall team speed," Bullington expressed a certain skepticism as to
whether his team could repeat as LSC and national champions in 1974.
"Gosh, I don't know. We could do it again, but it would sure take some
doing. Some of these young guys we're bringing in would have to step
right in there." Peppered with more questions by reporters in the ACC
conference room, Bullington admitted, "The odds are against us."[8]

Doubts gripped the head coach after his signal caller Clint Longley left with a year's eligibility remaining to sign with the Dallas Cowboys of the National Football League (NFL). Longley's absence left the Wildcats with a deep void and uncertainty at the key quarterback position. In addition, punitive actions against Hubert Pickett and Chuck Lawson meant that two players pivotal to the team's success in 1973 would be unavailable to the Wildcats in the 1974 season. Pickett and Lawson, both "ruled ineligible because of disciplinary reasons," eliminated the depth ACC counted on at both the running back and defensive tackle positions.[9]

Notwithstanding ACC's deficiencies on offense and defense, the Wildcats kicked off the 1974 season with a convincing 27–10 win over State College of Arkansas (now the University of Central Arkansas in Conway). Cleotha Montgomery, "Wilbert's little brother," spurred the victory with a 64-yard punt return and a 58-yard kickoff return. "Confidence," he explained, "is the most important ingredient a runner can possess. All I need is one or two good blocks and I'm off." Older brother Wilbert chipped in with four touchdown runs.[10]

In ACC's next game against the University of Nebraska–Omaha, the Wildcats faced a 9–7 halftime deficit. After a rousing speech by Bullington, the Wildcats came out a rejuvenated team. Greg Stirman admitted, "We just kept stopping ourselves. In the dressing room at halftime though, we got mad and came out and played a lot better." Wilbert Montgomery—as usual—made the difference, accumulating 109 yards with three receptions and three touchdowns. When asked whether the Mavericks organized their game plan to stop him specifically, Montgomery responded, "They're just doing a lot more keying, that's all." When local reporters reminded Bullington that Barry Switzer called Joe Washington "the best running back in the land," ACC's head man responded, "Well I wouldn't trade Wilbert for Washington. Sure he's a great back, but Switzer just hasn't seen Wilbert—and I've seen Washington."[11] The 35–9 victory over the Mavericks erased all "doubts" about the Wildcats' prospects of repeating their sterling 1973 season.

The third game of the season against the Texas A&I Javelinas, however, humbled the Wildcats, as they turned the ball over six times and lost, 46–14. The thirty-two point loss was coach Bullington's worst defeat since taking the helm in 1969. Wilbert Montgomery and fellow running back 5'5" Roy Colvin each scored, but they were outdone by the Javelina backfield of Larry Collins and Don Hardeman. Collins ran for 128 yards and a score, while Hardeman plowed through the ACC defense for 159 yards on fifteen carries and a touchdown.[12] Even though the Wildcats bounced back against Southwest Texas State University (now Texas State University–San Marcos), 42–9[13], they subsequently dropped a 14–10 heartbreaker to their longtime rivals the Stephen F. Austin (SFA) Lumberjacks.[14] The loss to the Lumberjacks essentially knocked ACC out of the LSC race, confirming Bullington's prophecy about the odds against repeating as both LSC and national champions.

Knowing that they were now playing for pride for the rest of the season, the Wildcats unleashed their wrath against the East Texas State University (ETSU) Lions before a home crowd of 12,500. ACC routed the Lions 31–13 as Wilbert rushed for 102 yards and two touchdowns; his brother Cleo put the Lions out of their misery after he sprinted 88 yards for the final score. Continuing his custom after every home win, Greg Stirman led the Big Purple Band in their victory song. Journalist Mark McDonald observed, "No Leonard Bernstein, but a tight end par excellence, Greg Stirman, has fostered a tradition of leaving the playing field, stumbling up the steps in his spikes to lead the ACC musicmakers."[15]

Riding high off their home win against ETSU, the Wildcats prevailed over their next four opponents. Without the services of their star ball carrier Wilbert Montgomery, the Wildcats easily handled the Sul Ross State University (SRSU) Lobos, 21–9[16], but their contest against the Angelo State University (ASU) Rams proved much more challenging. In the first half the Wildcats, behind the nifty running of Montgomery, jumped out to a 20–0 lead before a shoulder injury knocked Wilbert out of the game. The Rams then came roaring back to take a 21–20 lead. With Cleo Montgomery replacing his injured brother and rushing for 125 yards on seventeen carries, the Wildcats pulled out a 33–21 win. The ACC defense made a pivotal contribution, as John Isom, a Brownwood Lions product, recorded six unassisted tackles and Ray Nunez, a fierce 5'11", 210-pound freshman and state champion linebacker from Odessa Permian, leveled fourteen runners, recovered a Ram fumble to set up the go-ahead touchdown, and earned defensive Player of the Week honors.[17] The Wildcats then mauled the Tarleton State University (TSU) Texans, 56–14[18], and the Sam Houston State University (SHSU) Bearkats, 33–24.[19]

The last game of the 1974 season pitted the Wildcats against the Howard Payne University (HPU) Yellow Jackets. The previous year ACC soundly defeated their Brownwood foes 42–14 before advancing on to the

NAIA championship game, but an improved and determined Yellow Jacket team vowed revenge.[20] And they did. Forcing a remarkable eight Wildcat turnovers—five fumbles and three interceptions—the Yellow Jackets stung ACC, 42–21, before three thousand fans at Brownwood. HPU head coach Dean Slayton tried to rub the defeat in ACC's face by attempting a 27-yard field goal on the game's last play. The Wildcats were "bitter" about the loss[21], prompting reporter Mark McDonald's comment, "It was a bizarre turn of events that saw ACC go from champs to also-rans, so maybe eight Wildcat turnovers in the final game was appropriate. Not a humorous ending, but a symbolic one."[22]

ACC's 1974 season, then, proved deeply disappointing. The descent from champs to also-rans stemmed, however, not merely from on-the-field miscues. Off-the-field issues also demoralized the Wildcats. Earlier that spring, Clint Longley, ACC's premier quarterback, gave up his last year of eligibility to try out for the Dallas Cowboys. Shortly thereafter, ACC administrators expelled for the entire season both 6'3", 250-pound defensive lineman Chuck Lawson and hard-nosed runner and blocker Hubert Pickett for undisclosed inappropriate conduct. In October NAIA officials in Kansas informed ACC that they had to forfeit their win against State College of Arkansas for using a player who transferred to ACC with too few credits.[23] The Wildcats lost a game on paper that they had won on the field, giving them a respectable, yet still disappointing 7–4 season.

Aside from these distractions, opposing defensive coordinators, the lack of an effective Wildcat passing attack, and Wilbert Montgomery's physical maladies dampened ACC's season. By taming ACC's most valuable player, foes also subdued the entire Wildcat team as Montgomery drew attention from defenses, in the words of sports writer Mark McDonald, "from the time he stepped off the bus." An impaired shoulder limited Montgomery's play against ASU and HPU and kept him completely out of games against SRSU, TSU, and SHSU, so that Montgomery "never totally demoralized a defense as he had done the year before."[24] Beyond all this, Montgomery's early season clash with teammate Gary Graham sent shockwaves through the ACC community. Wildcats fans came to realize that Montgomery was certainly gifted athletically yet fully human in all respects.

"He's For Real, When He's Well": Wilbert Montgomery and the Abilene Christian Wildcats in 1975

[Wilbert Montgomery] only knows one gear—full speed.

Wally Bullington (quoted in Bill Hart, "Good Old No. 28," *Abilene Reporter News*, March 14, 1975)

E ven after the Wildcats' lackluster showing during the 1974 gridiron season, local sports writers stayed abreast of happenings on the Abilene Christian College (ACC) campus, especially concerning the activities of Wilbert Montgomery. Shortly after the Downtown Athletic Club in New York City awarded the 1974 Heisman Trophy to Ohio State Buckeye running back Archie Griffin, a writer had chided *Abilene Reporter News* sports writer Art Lawler for intimating that Montgomery was better than Griffin. Lawler replied, "Wilbert is better than anybody. There may be folks up in Ohio who don't realize this just yet, but in time, they'll learn. For anyone living in this area not to know Wilbert is No. 1—well that's inexcusable."[1]

During spring football practice in 1975, Wally Bullington watched his offense sputter repeatedly before yelling, "Gimme that unit we started with." The new group included Wilbert Montgomery, who quickly popped through the Wildcats' defense for ACC's only touchdown for the day. Assisting Bullington was Wayne Walton, a Wildcat alumnus then playing with the Kansas City Chiefs. Walton remarked that Montgomery was "better than anything we've got now. He's got more moves than Woody Green has."[2] Green, a native of Warren, Oregon, played collegiately at Arizona State University before being drafted in the first round by the Kansas City Chiefs. Shortly thereafter, with track season underway, Wilbert Montgomery and fellow footballer Johnny Perkins helped the ACC track team run a 42.9 at the West Texas Relays "despite not really working out on anything except a few handoffs."[3] These references to Montgomery in three different articles suggest that even after football season, he still occupied everybody's mind in the Abilene sports community.

When the Wildcats got down to the business of football in the fall, one hundred players reported for two-a-day workouts.[4] Within days that number decreased slightly, when three dropped out. Rusty Breazeale, a linebacker from Odessa Permian, enrolled at the University of Texas to study engineering; Tim Botkin, a wide receiver from Lubbock, decided to stay closer to home and attend Texas Tech University; Dean Low, a sophomore quarterback from Brownwood, had an emergency appendectomy and reported late.[5] Despite these and other substantive losses, Bullington seemed excited about the upcoming season, stating, "Everyday we're executing better. We have young players that are really learning more everyday what we're trying to do. There's constant improvement."[6] Bullington was especially enthusiastic about competing against a formidable first opponent, Troy State University.

Armed with a premier receiving unit, led by Perry Griggs, the Trojans were expected to finish near the top of the Gulf Coast Conference (GCC).[7] The ACC Wildcats, however, hammered the Trojans, 34–7, behind the laser-sharp passing of Jim Reese and the potent running of Wilbert Montgomery, who rushed for 101 yards, caught three passes for 42 more yards, and scored three touchdowns. Cleo helped finish off the Trojans by hauling in seven passes for 103 yards and a touchdown.[8] Tight end Greg Stirman's five receptions moved him over the hundred-catch mark, and one went for a 58-yard touchdown, "not bad for a blue-collar tight end."[9] Hard-hitting linebacker Ray Nunez spearheaded the Wildcats' defense with two forced fumbles, and sports writer Art Lawler joked that Nunez and "his surprisingly effective defensive teammates, were awarded extra chicken and oranges on the flight back to Abilene. Dick Felts did a bit of panhandling, and sympathetic Wildcat backers came forth with chicken legs for the po' 'lil 'ol boys in the back of the plane."[10] Having won their initial 1975 gridiron contest easily, the Wildcats enjoyed a jubilant plane ride home.

The day after their return, however, the team's joy faded. After football practice on Monday, September 15, an ACC student playfully sprayed Wilbert Montgomery with a water gun. Montgomery sternly warned the student not to do it again, but he did. Montgomery suddenly struck the white student in the mouth, cutting his lip. "The blow required three stitches," reported Garvin Beauchamp, ACC's vice president of student affairs.[11] The ACC administration suspended the star athlete from school for one day, but the college's judicial board, consisting of three faculty members and three students, voted to reinstate Montgomery.[12]

Shortly after the incident, rumors swirled across the ACC's campus and throughout the Abilene community. One rumor claimed that the review board voted to kick Montgomery out of school, but ACC president John C. Stevens "intervened and overruled it." Another story, equally erroneous, reported that African American football players boycotted practice "to show their loyalty to Wilbert." The reticence of ACC officials to issue public comments about the affair only contributed to the pervasiveness of the rumors. Frustrated over the prevailing gossip, sports journalist Bill Hart pierced through the false stories and correctly observed simply, "Wilbert Montgomery is a fine football player, a superstar in a small college, and as a result, whatever he does has a bit more significance than the average student or the average athlete. And good or bad, it's news."[13]

Even though racial upheaval shook several predominantly white university campuses across America in the 1960s[14], the Montgomery case was an isolated incident, neither racially motivated nor enduringly divisive. Montgomery and the other student, according to ACC officials, had a "good feeling toward each other"[15], and Montgomery recently recalled his aggressive behavior as a "reaction to a reaction," insisting that he was just exhausted from football practice and he failed to see the humor in being sprayed by a water gun.[16]

Knowing that the Wildcats were next scheduled to face their toughest LSC foe, the Texas A&I Javelinas, ACC officials and students alike certainly understood that they had little chance of defeating their south Texas opponents without Wilbert Montgomery. By briefly suspending but quickly reinstating their star running back, ACC's administration showed that they wanted to win and it could be argued that they allowed their star considerable latitude. Although Wilbert Montgomery appeared "by nature a peaceful sort," he obviously had a fiery temper and a penchant to unleash a fury at the blink of an eye. English professor David Merrell recalled the water gun incident, poignantly stating, "Wilbert Montgomery overreacted, but he didn't know what else to do. He responded inappropriately, but he was not the blame." He possessed a lot of "pent-up stuff . . . anger." "Students who played with him," Merrell explained, "knew not to cross him." Odis Dolton, a black athlete from Greenville, Mississippi, who followed Montgomery to West Texas, knew him well and cautioned that Wilbert was extremely shy and meek, but he could be aggressive when pushed too far. "Don't misunderstand his meekness," Dolton cautioned. "There was a monster in there. [Wilbert Montgomery] was not fearful, but one to be feared."[17]

Notwithstanding the resolution of this incident, Montgomery's 1975 season fell short of everyone's goals. Montgomery found reconciliation with the Wildcat community, but he was often injured and his on-the-field productivity dwindled. The Wildcats lost Wilbert along with several other pivotal players during the 1975 campaign, and finished their season 6–3–1.

Playing before a packed house of 15,000 in Shotwell Stadium, Montgomery gave up a costly fumble to A&I Javelinas defensive lineman Larry Seidel, who stripped Montgomery of the ball at the ACC 10-yard line. Two plays later quarterback Richard Ritchie handed off to running back Larry Collins, who dashed into the end zone from 6 yards out with 5:30 left in the game. Collins's touchdown gave the Javelinas the 24–21 victory. ACC's school newspaper, the *Optimist*, lamented the "heartbreaker" because it ruined the Wildcats' chance at a LSC championship. Montgomery finished the game with only 32 rushing yards.[18]

In spite of the wrenching loss to Texas A&I, the Wildcats looked optimistically toward their game against the 0–2 Southwest Texas State University Bobcats from San Marcos. In 1973 ACC had blasted the Bobcats, 42–9, and the following year the Wildcats had returned the favor, winning 41–7.[19] In the 1975 contest, however, the Bobcats "established superiority early" and never relinquished it. Despite Wilbert Montgomery's two touchdowns, the Bobcats outrushed the Wildcats 344 to 194 and defeated ACC, 21–16.[20] Montgomery managed to score career touchdowns number fifty-nine and sixty as well as surpass the 2,000-yard mark, but his team's loss soured any personal achievements.

The following week the Wildcats snapped their two-game losing streak by pounding the Stephen F. Austin (SFA) Lumberjacks, 24–3. Although the Wildcats won the contest, they lost their most valuable player; Montgomery, after catching a Jim Reese twenty-five yard touchdown pass, took a hard lick to the leg and had to sit out the remainder of the contest. Cleo Montgomery also suffered a serious knee injury, and Roy Carroll left the game with a separated shoulder. Sports editor Bill Hart quipped, "How costly the win was, only the doctors know."[21]

The injuries to Wildcat players mounted, after offensive lineman Mark Condra suffered a broken hand, center Don Wright had a sore toe, linebacker Ray Nunez hurt his shoulder, offensive guard Garry Moore came down with a virus, and receiver Johnny Perkins tore cartilage in his rib cage. Coach Wally Bullington yet believed that his Wildcats would make a strong showing against their next opponent, the ETSU Lions. "We all hate it," expressed Bullington with a mixture of realism and optimism, "but we can't do much about the injuries. I really feel like, however, our team will make a good effort against East Texas State. I think the kind of spirit they've shown this week and the kind of character I think they have, will really help us."[22] Notwithstanding Bullington's tempered optimism, the Wildcats had no answer for the Lions' running back Aundra Thompson, who ran for 209 yards on thirty-three carries and two touchdowns. The Lions defeated the Wildcats, 20–18, after ACC suffered two unsportsmanlike penalties and gave up six costly turnovers.[23]

After suffering another disappointing defeat, the wounded Wildcats brought a 2–3 record into their homecoming game against the Sul Ross Lobos. Because an injury once again prevented Wilbert Montgomery from playing, reporter Bill Hart observed, "Wilbert's a junior and for the third straight year he won't suit out for a Homecoming contest. But really, exes, he's for real when he's well." Cleo Montgomery, Gary Stirman, and Mike Lively suffered serious leg injuries, joining Wilbert on the sideline during the homecoming game. Other injured Wildcats included Ron McMullin (shoulder), Roy Carroll (shoulder), Mark Condra (wrist), Clint Owens (ankle), Chuck Lawson (shoulder), Ray Nunez (shoulder), and Kevin McLeod (leg).[24]

With several ailing starters out, other leaders stepped up and had a big game before ten thousand fans huddled in chilly Shotwell Stadium.

Quarterback Jim Reese led the Wildcat assault on the Lobos, completing eight out of fourteen passes for 247 yards and two touchdowns. Even though Johnny Perkins hauled in only four passes, they covered 176 yards, as Hubert Pickett helped out the ground attack with 115 yards on nineteen carries. After the 49–14 homecoming victory over Sul Ross, standout tight end Greg Stirman again stood before the Big Purple Band and led the "La Grandoso March" as the players and fans exited the stadium.[25]

Wilbert Montgomery returned to the Wildcats' lineup for the next game against the ASU Rams, but could not go at full speed. The Rams' smothering defense limited Montgomery to 22 yards on six carries, leaving him scoreless for the first time in his collegiate career. After Harold Nutall recovered a Rams fumble at the 41-yard line, quarterback Jim Reese hit receiver Ike O'Bryant for a 19-yard strike with thirteen seconds remaining. Quickly regaining the ball, the Wildcats ran a draw play which Hubert Pickett amazingly carried "all the way to the one foot line." With five seconds left, ACC felt certain that kicker Jay Reeves would clinch the ball game with a chip-shot field goal, but Rams defender James Cross flew across the line, blocked the kick, and preserved a 17–17 tie.[26]

The Wildcats bounced back the following week against the Tarleton Texans, as a healthier Wilbert Montgomery flashed the best rushing performance of his collegiate career. With 213 rushing yards and 32 receiving yards, Montgomery sparked the Wildcats to their fourth win of the season. Bill Hart described his longest run of the day: "Wilbert's longest run was a 46 yarder, a typical Montgomery effort. He broke tackle after tackle, but too many Texans kept him from going all the way." ACC won the game, 35–21, but suffered still more injuries to other key players. Greg Stirman tore ligaments in his knee, Ray Nunez left the game with a sprained ankle, and Ron McMullin's season ended with yet another injury.[27]

ACC rolled past their next opponent Sam Houston State, 55–20, as a healthy Wilbert Montgomery ignited the effort. "Wilbert Montgomery," explained Bill Hart, "did more things in the first half for Abilene Christian College Saturday night than most players do in a season as he sparked the Wildcats to a 55–20 victory over Sam Houston State. The junior tailback scored three touchdowns, one on a 99-yard punt return, and also threw his first touchdown pass of the year before retiring to the bench."[28] Montgomery's feats ran his career touchdown total to sixty-six and again earned him LSC Player of the Week honors.[29]

ACC played its last football game of 1975 against archrival Howard

Payne University Yellow Jackets. The previous year saw the Yellow Jackets blister the ACC, 42–21, and players well remembered that the Yellow Jackets stopped the clock in the closing seconds of the game to attempt a field goal, despite holding a comfortable lead.[30] Coach Bullington predicted, "It'll be an emotional game. It's similar to the Dallas Cowboys and the Washington Redskins game, or the Texas Longhorns and the Texas Aggies—on a different scale."[31]

Emotions did indeed run high as the Wildcats crushed the Yellow Jackets, 45–14. Art Lawler called the contest "an ACC feast" as the Reese-Perkins connection obliterated the opposing defense. The ACC signal caller completed nineteen out of thirty-seven passes for 313 yards and three touchdowns as Johnny Perkins collected ten of Reese's tosses for 185 yards, eclipsing the LSC all-time single season receiving record. Lawler added that the Wildcats showed little mercy, and in fact probably got a little too greedy—Reese suffered three interceptions while trying to go for more "home runs." Wilbert Montgomery added 61 yards on twenty-one carries and two touchdowns. Ray Nunez and the Wildcat defense stifled the Yellow Jackets' attack, limiting them to 290 total yards. Nunez became so emotionally charged that officials ejected him from the game "for being a central figure in a fourth-quarter brawl."[32] Players from both teams ran out onto the field and jabbed at each other, and Bill Hart reported that HPU's cheerleaders even verbally sparred with Wildcat players.[33] Despite the ruckus the Wildcats tasted sweet revenge.

Given their 1973 championship season standard, the ACC Wildcats finished their 1975 campaign deeply disappointed. After an impressive win over the Troy State Trojans in Dothan, Alabama, the Wildcats seemed poised to return to prominence. However, Wilbert Montgomery's retaliation against an ACC student shook up the campus and the broader Abilene community, reminding Wilbert's admirers that while he was a remarkably gifted athlete, his explosive temper underscored his complete humanness.

Furthermore, Montgomery's own injuries kept him out of games against the ETSU Lions and the SRSU Lobos and restricted his action in other pivotal games. The injury bug bit other key Wildcat players. Cleotha Montgomery, Ted Sitton, and Greg Stirman all suffered season-ending injuries, and several other first-line players lost significant game time, assuring ACC's fifth-place finish in the LSC. Perhaps the brightest spot in the Wildcats' 1975 was the emergence of future NFL receiver Johnny Perkins, who earned first team all LSC honors.[34] Art Lawler called Perkins "Superman. That is to say, he borrowed Wilbert Montgomery's uniform, stretched it over his 6–3 frame, and disguised himself as a mild-mannered split end on a struggling ballclub."[35] Significantly, Lawler measured Perkins's success beside ACC's pole star and standard bearer, Wilbert Montgomery. Despite ACC's challenges, devastating injuries, and frustrations in 1975, Abilene observers knew that their real superstar was Wilbert Montgomery. As sports journalist Bill Hart so succinctly put it, "He's for real, when he's well."

Broken Bones, Broken Hearts, and Broken Records: Wilbert Montgomery and the Abilene Christian Wildcats in 1976

[Wilbert] Montgomery, ACU's all-time rushing leader, is a quiet young man who does his talking with a football cradled in one arm. One of the most gifted runners in the nation, Montgomery moves with gazelle-like quickness.

Ron Hadfield (quoted in "Davis Learns from Montgomery," *Optimist*, November 19, 1976)

n 1976 the United States commemorated its bicentennial and elected its thirty-ninth president, Jimmy Carter, the first chief executive from the Deep South in half a century.[1] The national enthusiasm generated by the bicentennial celebration spilled over into the Abilene community as Abilene Christian College (ACC) became Abilene Christian University (ACU) and its enrollment soared to a record high of 3,979 students.[2] In this exciting and changing milieu, Wilbert Montgomery finished his collegiate career as a Wildcat, and because of his presence at ACU, the Wildcats once again entered the 1976 football season with high expectations. But a mixture of trials and triumphs, setbacks and successes were to mark this season.

Before a home crowd of 8,500 fans, ACU blew out its first opponent, the Northwestern Oklahoma State University (NWOSU) Rangers, 48–14, behind Wilbert Montgomery's two rushing touchdowns. The Wildcats took command of the game in the first half and never looked back, even though starting quarterback Jim Reese and all-conference receiver Johnny Perkins saw limited action because of injuries.[3]

The Wildcats' second foe, the University of Northern Colorado (UNC) Bears, proved to be much more challenging. After a 7–7 halftime tie, the Bears pulled ahead when UNC's defensive back Bob Curry picked off a Jim Reese pass and returned it 48 yards for a score. The Wildcats' defense, determined to make up for last week's "lazy" performance, came to the rescue. Defensive back, Duff Phipps, intercepted two of UNC quarterback Russ Boone's passes in the fourth quarter, helping to seal the victory. The first pick set up Hubert Pickett's 7-yard touchdown run, the game clincher. The second one in the last eleven seconds of the game closed out a 21–14 triumph.[4] Pickett scored all three touchdowns for ACU; Wilbert Montgomery left the game in the fourth quarter with a deep thigh bruise. Ron Hadfield, sports writer for ACU's school newspaper, captured how fans felt about their star athlete despite his miscues and injuries.

> Montgomery, the workhorse of the Wildcat offense, had a tough night. Though he fumbled twice, it must be made known that he played with a bad right thigh and several shots from the UNC defense which left him so groggy that he had to be assisted to the locker room in the fourth quarter. Wilbert is a tremendous competitor, and showed it as he ground out 50 tough yards in several clutch situations.[5]

ACU's third game of the 1976 season came against Lone Star Conference powerhouse, Texas A&I. Having lost the two previous contests to the Javelinas, the Wildcats vowed revenge. Before a crowd of seventeen thousand the two teams played to a 10–10 tie at intermission; Javelinas quarterback Richard Ritchie "killed the Wildcats with his flawless execution on the option plays" and generated twenty-eight second half points, leading A&I to a 38–10 rout. Cleo Montgomery scored ACU's only touchdown with an 8-yard reception from quarterback Jim Reese. Cleo's brother garnered 80 rushing yards but gave up a crucial fumble that helped widen the Javelinas' lead.[6]

Wilbert Montgomery striking a pose for the ACC Wildcats, 1976. Courtesy of Abilene Christian University.

Ray Nunez, ACU's outstanding linebacker, suffered a severe ankle injury during the course of the game. As he tried to leave the field, Nunez stumbled, fell, and "stood up in an attempt to get to the sidelines, but fell face down after limping a few feet. Before anyone could react to help him, he tried again to reach the bench, but collapsed and nearly crawled the remaining few feet." The usually energetic and prideful Nunez then "put his head in his hands and wept." His pain and agony prompted jeers and cheers from the hostile Javelinas crowd. Hadfield, dubbing their reaction "childish" and "disgusting," added, "Football in Kingsville is brutal." He then urged ACU fans not to imitate the Javelinas' example but instead to show the "proper attitude in both victory and defeat."[7]

ACU experienced more emotional and physical pain the following week in their loss against the Southwest Texas State Bobcats, the same team that defeated them a year earlier. Turnovers and penalties doomed the Wildcats, and coach Wally Bullington benched fullback Hubert Pickett after he "fumbled on two straight carries," replacing him with freshman running back Kelly Kent, who ran for 45 yards on only six carries. Wilbert Montgomery kept the game interesting with his 3-yard scamper for a Wildcat touchdown, but a miscue between senior quarterback Jim Reese and freshman receiver Ricky Lewis in the closing seconds sealed ACU's second loss of the season. Art Lawler captured the game well by observing that "Southwest Texas turned in a carbon copy of last year's upset by nailing the Wildcats by the same score, 21–16."[8]

After the emotional loss to SWTSU, the *Abilene Reporter News* delineated the number of Wildcat players with injuries, calling it a list long "enough to make you cry." Wilbert Montgomery, Alex Davis, Terry Merck, Mark McCurley, and Greg Newman grappled with knee injuries. Montgomery and Ricky Felts also nursed hurt shoulders while Johnny Perkins struggled to overcome his hamstring injury. Cleo Montgomery suffered with an injured finger, and Ray Nunez had a chipped bone in his foot. Felts, Merck, Davis, Nunez, and McCurley were all ruled out of the impending matchup with the Stephen F. Austin Lumberjacks, while Perkins and the Montgomery brothers were declared probable. With a tinge of humor the *Abilene Reporter News* listed the entire ACU coaching staff, Wally Bullington, Ted Sitton, Don Smith, Jerry Wilson, and Bob Strader as those with "broken hearts."[9]

Broken bones and broken hearts notwithstanding, ACU traveled to Nacogdoches and bounced back in a major way, pounding the Lumberjacks, 51–14. In spite of leg and shoulder injuries, Wilbert Montgomery rushed for a season high 137 yards and one touchdown, tying the national collegiate career touchdown record. Brother Cleo contributed with an 8-yard touchdown reception, as did Johnny Perkins, whose 40-yard catch gave him his first six points of the season.[10]

Excitement and anxiety pervaded the ACU campus as the Wildcats prepared for homecoming game against ETSU. Wildcats fans knew that Wilbert Montgomery was close to breaking the NCAA touchdown record, and the players shared the anticipation.[11] The day before the home-coming game Montgomery told ACU's kicker Ove Johansson that he was one touchdown away from a national scoring record, and Johansson, a former soccer player from Sweden, responded, "If I get a shot at it, I'm going to set a national kicking record."[12]

On October 16, 1976, a windy Saturday afternoon, thirteen thousand avid Wildcats supporters witnessed the fall of three NCAA marks. First, Montgomery carried the ball twenty-one times for 120 yards and one touchdown, breaking Walter Payton's NCAA touchdown record. Next, Montgomery eclipsed ACU's total rushing record, a standard previously set by V. T. Smith from 1946 and 1948. Montgomery's performance against the Lions gave him 2,586 career rushing yards; Smith, later in the NFL, had ended his career at ACC with 2,535 yards. No one in Shotwell Stadium expected to see another record broken that day, yet with 2:13 left to play in the first quarter, Bullington sent out Johansson to attempt a 69-yard field goal. Despite a high snap from center, Johansson, the beneficiary of a tail wind, hit the ball perfectly and it sailed through the goalpost with 3 yards to spare. Sports writer Art Lawler captured the atmosphere of Shotwell Stadium after Johansson's kick: "The previous[sic] quiet crowd of 13,000 erupted in celebration and the Wildcat bench emptied onto the field smothering Johansson with congratulations as the official beneath the goal post raised his arms high in the air."[13]

Baffled by all of the excitement and commotion, Johansson failed to realize the significance of the feat and yelled, confused, "Does it really count?" A writer from the *Abilene Reporter News* asked of Johansson in the third quarter, "Did you do anything different this morning than usual?" The Swedish kicker retorted jokingly, "Well, I ate a bigger breakfast than usual."[14]

ACU quarterback Jim Reese joined his teammates by breaking four records of his own during the Wildcats' next game against the Angelo State Rams. Reese completed twenty-six out of thirty-nine passes for a whopping 564 yards and two touchdowns; in so doing he not only led the Wildcats to a 26–0 win but he also surpassed the single-game school passing mark set by Clint Longley in 1973. He further wiped out a NAIA total passing record of 502 yards. Reese also raised his career passing yardage to 5,127, erasing the old standard of 5,027 set by Texas A&I's Karl Douglas between 1967 and 1970. Reese's amazing performance overshadowed Montgomery's 35 rushing yards and two touchdowns.[15] The victory over

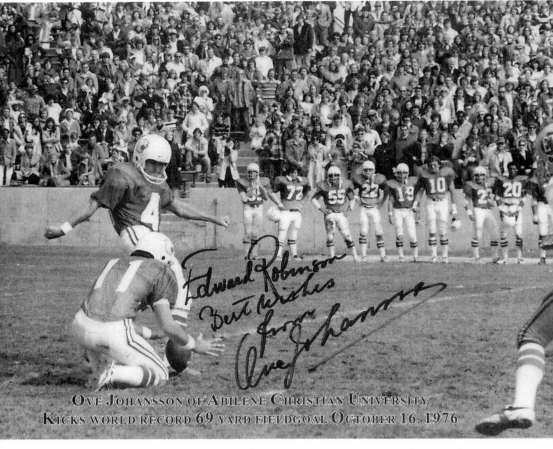

OVE JOHANSSON OF ABILENE CHRISTIAN UNIVERSITY
KICKS WORLD RECORD 69 YARD FIELDGOAL OCTOBER 16, 1976

Against East Texas State University (now Texas A & M University at Commerce), Ove Johansson, a native of Sweden, kicked a world record sixty-nine-yard field goal for the ACC Wildcats before thirteen thousand avid fans. Courtesy of Abilene Christian University.

the Angelo State Rams marked the last time Reese, Montgomery, and other seniors suited up in a Wildcat uniform in Shotwell Stadium.

While Jim Reese and the Wildcats offense put on an impressive aerial display against Angelo State, their defensive unit, led by Ray Nunez and John Usrey, shone even more brightly. Unlike the intense and boisterous Nunez, Usrey, a business major from Lakewood, Colorado, was more subdued, choosing to play football at ACU because it was a good school with a "Christian environment."[16] Despite their different personalities, Usrey and Nunez became close friends and roommates who relished pounding their opponents on the field. This linebacking duo helped ACU produce three straight shutouts, blanking Angelo State, 26–0; Cameron State, 42–0; and Sam Houston State, 26–0.[17]

ACU's contest against the Cameron University Aggies marked Wilbert Montgomery's last game as a Wildcat. On his sixth carry of the game, for his 99th yard, Montgomery went down hard and suffered a deep thigh bruise, never returning to the game or to the field in a Wildcats uniform. Despite his season-ending injury, Montgomery assumed the responsibility of mentoring freshman running back Alex Davis, a 5'9", 170-pound speedster known to his teammates as "A. D.," and a 1,300-yard rusher at his high school in central Texas.[18] In ACU's season finale Davis, with strong support from veterans Jim Reese, Johnny Perkins, and Hubert Pickett, among others, led the defeat of archrival Howard Payne University, 34–14, earning the Wildcats a berth in the Shrine Bowl in Pasadena, Texas.[19]

Mixed emotions swirled about the ACU campus leading up to the Shrine Bowl against "that other" Church of Christ school—Harding College. On the one hand, ACU fans were thrilled to follow their Wildcats into the postseason; on the other hand, they understood that they would be without their star player, Wilbert Montgomery. Before taking to the field Reuben Mason, a 6'2", 205-pound linebacker, took the floor in the locker room and gave an emotional speech:

> Every one of you know how Wil has been looking the past few days, and we know how much he wanted to play in this game. But he's played his last game with us. All I want to say is—if we play today like Wil has always played for us, we won't have any problem winning.[20]

After Mason's heartfelt speech, the emotional and teary eyed Wildcats charged onto the field before a crowd of almost eight thousand spectators and thrashed the Bisons, 22–12. Quarterback Jim Reese picked apart the Harding defense for 311 yards and earned the game's Outstanding Offensive Player award. Freshman Alex Davis ran for 96 yards and caught five passes for 71 more. All-America receiver Johnny Perkins collected eleven passes for 156 yards and a touchdown.[21]

Even though Wilbert Montgomery never played a down in the Shrine Bowl, his mere presence in the Wildcats' locker room and on the sideline profoundly inspired his teammates. Sports writer Ron Hadfield offered a fitting tribute: "All of us owe a great deal of thanks to Wilbert, whose four-year stay at ACU is a touching story. He's been through difficult times that only those who know him well can understand."[22] Many people knew of Montgomery's athletic abilities, but few knew his challenges and struggles as a black athlete in a predominantly white context. Wilbert Montgomery appeared to be superhuman, yet he was fully human—a black man with real pain, real joys, and real sorrows.

Ups and downs, trials and triumphs, and successes and struggles, then, marked Wilbert Montgomery's tenure at ACU. Transitioning from the Mississippi Delta to West Texas meant that Montgomery went from a black majority world to a region where the number of minorities was small. Even though the Felts family and many others genuinely befriended him, Montgomery felt the sting of racism as he found himself restricted from certain restaurants in the Abilene community. Randy Scott, Montgomery's classmate, remembered that the black athletes from Mississippi who enrolled at ACC said that Texas was "like heaven to them" because race relations appeared to be more harmonious.[23] Texas might have appeared to have better race relations compared to Mississippi, but the Lone Star State was no racial paradise, even for talented black athletes. University of Houston's standout running back Warren McVea said that a few of his teammates and coaches refused to speak to him; and some UH students barraged him with racial slurs. Subtle racism disturbed John Westbrook at Baylor University, "a Christian school." Some University of Texas players spat on Southern Methodist University's Jerry LeVias and told him, "Go on back to your nigger mama." He also received death threats and hate mail, stating such things as "Boat ticket back to Africa."[24]

The playing days of Warren McVea, John Westbrook, and Jerry LeVias occurred in the mid-1960s, yet what was true for Baptist-controlled Baylor University and Methodist-affiliated SMU was unquestionably true for other church-related institutions, including Abilene Christian University. G. P. Holt, an influential black preacher in Churches of Christ, charged that white school administrators at Christian colleges admitted African American students, not because they wanted them, but because of pressure from the federal government. "We know and you know and God knows that our Colleges have not had a *Change of Heart*," Holt asserted in 1969, but the "Government of our land is responsible for" the few black students attending Church of Christ–affiliated colleges.[25] Thus, when Montgomery arrived on West Texas soil four years later, racial discrimination was still rife there and beyond. Randy Scott recalled white proprietors of a restaurant in Nacogdoches, Texas, throwing out black members of ACC's basketball team.[26]

In addition to emotional scars, multiple injuries beset Wilbert Montgomery: a separated shoulder, knee problems, and a deep thigh bruise. This explains why his rushing totals declined from 1,181 yards as a freshman to 657 as a sophomore, 612 as a junior, and 597 as a senior. His declining health and dwindling statistics caused many National Football League (NFL) scouts to spurn him; his stock dropped drastically in the 1977 NFL draft. Additionally, Montgomery left ACU without his college diploma. Despite leaving ACU without a degree, Montgomery's former teammate and classmate Bob Strader quickly defended him by noting that even though the university measures success in the attainment of degrees, Wilbert was still successful in that he "fulfilled the mission of the university without a degree."[27] Indeed, most African American footballers who followed Montgomery's path from Abilene to the NFL did not stay four years and never earned a degree from ACU.

Wilbert Montgomery, notwithstanding his failure to graduate, walked away with many regional and national honors as well as a national championship ring. He gave substantially to ACU as an athlete-student by helping to fill Shotwell Stadium, by leading other African American student-athletes from Mississippi to West Texas, and by raising money benefiting a handicapped organization in the Abilene community. Two months after Montgomery led the Wildcats to a national title, the *Abilene Reporter News* photographed the black athlete holding a handicapped girl, Julie Whigham, on his knee. It is clear that the organization, the Abilene Association for Retarded Children, used the local and national football star's popularity to raise proceeds for its cause.[28] Perhaps his greatest accomplishment, however, was that he helped change white people's perceptions of black people in this region. Abilene Christian University changed Wilbert Montgomery; Wilbert Montgomery in turn helped change Abilene Christian University as well as the community beyond.

Part III

Wilbert Montgomery in the
National Football League, 1977–1986

Chapter 8

Flying with the Eagles: Wilbert Montgomery in the National Football League

[Wilbert Montgomery's] the consummate team player. Some backs might run better, some might catch a little better, but no one does everything as well as he does.

Ron Jaworski (quoted in Ralph Bernstein, "Wilbert: 'I Never Thought I'd Make It," *Abilene Reporter News*, September 16, 1984)

[Wilbert] Montgomery is an excellent running back. He has great leg drive.... I don't know of anybody other than [Walter] Payton who has more ability in their legs than Montgomery. When you play against him, you better be tackling. If you're not, he's going to run for a lot of yardage.

Tom Landry (quoted in Bill Hart, "Wilbert Seeks a Cure for Fumblitis," *Abilene Reporter News*, November 12, 1979)

Drafted in the sixth round with the 154th pick by the Philadelphia Eagles, Wilbert Montgomery in the spring of 1977 packed his bags in Abilene, Texas, and headed north. Upon arriving in the City of Brotherly Love, Montgomery joined 1.7 million residents in a historically and culturally rich city. Black Philadelphians often boasted that their city was the birthplace of "Mother

Bethel," the African Methodist Episcopal Church, established by Richard Allen in 1791; the home of the *Philadelphia Tribune*, the oldest continuously running black paper in the United States; the adopted hometown of a creator of gospel music C. A. Tindley; the birthplace of renowned comedian and entertainer Bill Cosby; and home to Julius "Dr. J" Erving and the Philadelphia 76ers, who would bring their avid fans a National Basketball Association (NBA) championship in 1983.[1]

Wilbert was one of many African American athletes who transitioned from playing sports in the South to joining a professional team in the North. Walter Payton starred at Jackson State College in Mississippi before leading the Chicago Bears to a Super Bowl victory.[2] Linebacker Mike Singletary, a native of Houston, Texas, joined Payton and the Bears 1981 after a stellar career at Baylor University.[3] Mel Blount, from Vidalia, Georgia, and a standout defensive back at Southern University in Louisiana, helped the Pittsburgh Steelers win four Super Bowls during his career.[4] Charles Barkley excelled as a basketball player in Alabama before launching his all-star NBA career with Philadelphia 76ers.[5] Wilbert Montgomery followed this same path by enjoying a successful career in West Texas before moving on to Pennsylvania to play for the Eagles.

Black athletes who launched professional careers in the North soon learned of the ubiquity of racism in America. In 1957 Bill Russell, after a stellar collegiate career at the University of San Francisco, became a member of the Boston Celtics. Despite leading the Celtics to multiple championships, the city of Boston never fully embraced Russell, who was often miserable and "excluded from almost everything except practice and the games" because of his race. Thirteen years later Mel Blount said that a "new fear" gripped his heart as he walked onto the field for his first game in the NFL. "I was lost in a sea of white faces," recalled Blount. "I looked to the coaches for support, but all I could see were white faces. I had been thrown into a white world, and I didn't know my place." Later in his rookie year, after Blount gave up a forty-two yard touchdown to the Oakland Raiders' speedy receiver Cliff Branch, a Pittsburgh fan yelled, "Bench that stupid nigger!"[6]

Philadelphia 76er Charles Barkley, while driving his Porsche in the city, recalled being pulled over by police officers for "DWB—Driving While Black." He also felt that in certain parts of the City of Brotherly Love a black man was often "subjected to the Klan without the sheets," and that Philadelphia's media often displayed racist characteristics. Once when Barkley commented that the 76ers had to improve in order to advance in the playoffs, the press gave his words a negative twist: "BARKLEY BLASTS TEAMMATES!"[7]

Conversely, black athletes who played their college football in the North and transitioned to the South to play professionally also found themselves in the clutches of a different sort of racial discrimination. Tony Dorsett grew up in Aliquippa, Pennsylvania, starred for the Pittsburgh Panthers, and won the Heisman Trophy in 1976. Yet after the Dallas Cowboys picked him in the first round of the 1977 draft, Dorsett relocated from the Northeast to the South and experienced culture shock. "It was the first time in my life," Dorsett observed, "that I was exposed, on a daily basis, to the southern drawl, the slow pace of life, the conservatism, and the overt racism." Upon arriving in Dallas he found segregation pervasive; most blacks lived in South Dallas while most white resided in North Dallas. Whites in Tarrant County, Dorsett pointed out, "didn't seem to have a problem calling you a nigger right to your face. It wasn't that I hadn't been exposed to racial prejudice before in my life, but where I came from, if they took a chance and called you nigger, they'd be fifty yards away and running." Dorsett obviously encountered subtle racism in the North, but he faced a more overt and more emboldened brand of racism in the South. Historian Michael Phillips has pointed out that during the 1960s and 1970s "White flight also gripped Dallas." Businesses, including the Dallas Cowboys football team, followed the human exodus.[8] This is the racial milieu in which Dorsett lived and moved.

Tony Dorsett and Wilbert Montgomery finished their collegiate careers the same year, but the two running backs swapped states as professionals. Unlike Dorsett, who relocated from Pennsylvania to Texas, Montgomery transitioned from Texas to Pennsylvania; and like other black athletes who moved from the South to the North, Montgomery had brushes with white racists there. In his second season with the Eagles, Montgomery rode down Broad Street in his rented Dodge Aspen with two of his black teammates, Billy Campfield and Oren Middlebrook. Five white ruffians from South Philly, evidently angry because of the baseball Phillies ninth-inning loss to the Los Angeles Dodgers, pulled up beside Montgomery's car and spewed racial slurs at the three players. Accustomed to such invective, Montgomery and his passengers at first ignored them, but when the scoundrels hurled a wad of spit at them, they retaliated. Campfield and Middlebrook punched out two of the miscreants, while Montgomery han-

Wilbert Montgomery carrying the ball for the Philadelphia Eagles, c. 1979. Courtesy of Abilene Christian University.

dled two others, who "required hospital care." The fifth culprit absconded. After the incident, a reporter asked Montgomery whether the men were white, adding, "What did they look like?" Montgomery replied: "I don't know. They was all bloody."[9] Montgomery, while often seemingly meek and gentle, could unleash his explosive temper when pushed too far by racial harassment—whether in Texas or Pennsylvania.

But Wilbert Montgomery did not relocate to Pennsylvania to fight racial battles; he moved to make the Philadelphia Eagles football team. In the spring of 1977, Montgomery walked into the Eagles' training camp with a battered body, a wealth of athletic talent, and a determined heart. Yet doubt and uncertainty flooded his mind. He was unsure whether he would make the team, and as Eagles quarterback Ron Jaworski recalled, Montgomery kept a towel under his door during the first training camp to prevent a pink slip from getting underneath. Montgomery confessed that he had difficulty comprehending the Eagles' system. "Every night I studied harder and all I got was more confused. I'd sit in meetings and they would be using terms I'd never heard before. I was afraid to ask questions. I was afraid that they'd think I was dumb." He actually packed his bags the morning of every cut day. Head coach Dick Vermeil considered cutting Montgomery because he failed to "line up right, with all the formations and motion." Yet Vermeil knew that Montgomery possessed talent; he just required patience. "You see innate talent," Vermeil concluded, "and you tell yourself you've got to have time." In the closing years of his NFL career, Montgomery confessed that "I never thought I'd make it."[10]

Wilbert Montgomery did indeed make the Eagles' roster, and he immediately began winning over Philadelphia fans. One young admirer, Van Henry, a white teenager from Burlington, New Jersey, enrolled at ACU after reading about Montgomery's story in the *Philadelphia Inquirer*. Sports writer Gordon Forbes recounted Montgomery's "star-spangled" football career at ACU and asked him if he was upset that his teammate Johnny Perkins was chosen by the New York Giants in the second round, four rounds ahead of him. Montgomery replied, "I don't feel sore about that. I'm just glad the Lord gave me the opportunity and the Eagles picked me and gave me the opportunity to prove myself."[11]

But not until the last game of his rookie season against the New York Jets did Montgomery get his "small chance" to start and shine in the Eagles' backfield, rushing for 103 yards and two touchdowns as the Eagles defeated the Jets, 27–0. More importantly, Montgomery's performance presaged brighter days for the Eagles franchise, while erasing all doubts from Montgomery's mind as well as those of his critics who questioned his ability to play in the NFL. "That was all I needed," explained Montgomery. "That showed me I could cut it. The doubts I had about myself ended right there."[12]

During his sophomore season in the NFL, Montgomery picked up steam and mesmerized opponents with his shifty moves and tough running style. Even though the Eagles started the 1978 season 0–2, the team rebounded with a three-game winning streak, defeating the New Orleans Saints, 24–17, the Miami Dolphins, 17–3, and the Baltimore Colts, 17–14. Montgomery posted his first 100-plus-yard game in 1978 in the Superdome against the Saints, and he ran through Dolphin tacklers for 111 yards on twenty-five carries.[13] Against the Colts he rushed for 144 yards on twenty-five carries, scoring the game-winning touchdown late in the fourth quarter.[14] As Montgomery's numbers piled up, Philadelphia fans and sports writers started to take more notice of this singularly talented athlete from a small West Texas university. Local sports observers dubbed him "Wilbert the Wiz" because of his seemingly magical moves on the football field. "He's no Dorsett or Payton," explained Eagle coach Dick Vermeil, "but he's the best we've got. He could be to us what Terry Metcalf was to the Cardinals."[15]

Notwithstanding Montgomery's emergence as a featured NFL running back, he and the Eagles experienced a rollercoaster 1978 season. After their victory over the Colts, they lost to the New England Patriots before bouncing back against the Washington Redskins, 17–10. At home against the Redskins, Montgomery chalked up 125 yards on twenty-five carries, but the Eagles then lost back-to-back games against conference foes, Dallas and St. Louis. Following the loss to the Cardinals, the Eagles reeled off four straight wins against the Green Bay Packers, 10–3, the New York Jets, 17–9, the New York Giants, 19–17, and the St. Louis Cardinals, 14–10.

The highlight of the Eagles' 1978 season came against the New York Giants, not once but twice. On November 19 Montgomery and the Eagles experienced "The Miracle at the Meadowlands." In the closing moments of the game, the Eagles had no timeouts; the Giants had the ball and the lead, 17–12. Instead of simply taking a knee to end the game, however, Giant quarterback Joe Pisarcik tried to hand off the ball to Larry Csonka. The ball popped loose, and Eagle defensive back Herman Edwards scooped it up, dashed into the end zone, and won the game, 19–17, keeping alive the Eagles' playoff hopes.[16]

A few weeks later, the Eagles' last game of the season was at home against the same New York Giants, and a victory would give Philadelphia a playoff slot. Wilbert Montgomery slashed through the Giant defense for two touchdowns and 120 yards on twenty-five carries, giving him a total of 1,220 yards. This mark broke a twenty-nine-year-old Eagles' single-season career rushing record, set by Hall of Famer Steve Van Buren in 1949. After the game Van Buren visited the Eagles' locker room and gave Montgomery high praise: "There are only two runners in your class, you and Walter Payton."[17] More significantly, because the Los Angeles Rams knocked off the Green Bay Packers, the Eagles clinched a playoff berth for the first time since 1960—and their first winning record since 1966.[18]

Wilbert Montgomery running, fulfilling a lifelong dream of playing professional football for the Philadelphia Eagles. Courtesy of Alex Zerkel of the Philadelphia Eagles.

The Eagles' 1978 season ended, however, on a bittersweet note. On the one hand, a stingy Atlanta Falcons defense bottled up Montgomery for just nineteen yards on sixteen carries, knocking off the Eagles, 14–13. On the other hand, the Eagles knew that they had a rising star in Montgomery, who earned a spot on the All-Pro Team. During the annual Pro Bowl in Los Angeles, Montgomery led the NFC in rushing and to a 13–7 victory over the AFC, even though Minnesota Vikings receiver Ahmad Rashad garnered Most Valuable Player honors. Montgomery, after being reunited with some college acquaintances such as Walter Payton of Jackson State and Thomas "Hollywood" Henderson of Langston on the NFC Team, called his participation in the Pro Bowl game a "great experience for me because I got to be with some of the top ball players."[19] To reward Montgomery's brilliant season, Eagles general manager Jim Murray signed him to a five-year contract reportedly worth $1.5 million.[20] Montgomery delighted in receiving such personal recognition and rewards, but he yearned most intensely for an improved Eagles team and a better season in 1979.

Buoyed by an improved defense, a more refined passing game, and the running exploits of Wilbert Montgomery, the 1979 Philadelphia Eagles got off to a 6–1 start. Their fifth win of the season had come at home against Washington, as Montgomery blistered the Redskins' defense for 127 yards and four touchdowns on twenty-two carries.[21] After the sound defeat of Washington, coach Dick Vermeil stood before reporters "all smiles," predicting that if the Eagles played "up to our ability we can beat them all. But the only thing we can do right now is get ready for St. Louis next Sunday."[22] The following week the Eagles extended their winning streak to five games, with a 24–20 triumph over the Cardinals, boosting their season record to 6–1. Montgomery again led with 117 rushing yards and one touchdown.[23]

Three consecutive losses, however, brought the Eagles back to earth. The Redskins got revenge, 17–7, while the Cincinnati Bengals pummeled them, 37–13; next the Cleveland Browns rallied in the last minute to win 24–19. The contest against the Browns was especially difficult for Montgomery, who rushed for 197 yards and a touchdown, but gave up a costly fumble, enabling Cleveland to get back into the game.[24]

Montgomery's feats had not gone unnoticed by his alma mater, and ACU officials decided to honor him on a Sunday afternoon before an important Monday night game against the Dallas Cowboys in Texas Stadium. University president John C. Stevens presented him with an Alumni Citation Award (currently called "Distinguished Alumni: Citation") in recognition of his athletic prowess as a former ACU student-athlete and as a budding star for the Philadelphia Eagles. At the Marriott Hotel in Dallas, Eagles head coach Dick Vermeil took the podium to say,

We get so intense as coaches, we sometimes forget the players are human. We shouldn't let things like this get distorted. I tell Wilbert to never forget how he got where he is. No coach loves a player as I do Wilbert. He's in a class with the top five running backs in the league.[25]

Vermeil expressed gratitude to Wilbert not just for his athletic skill, but also for his attitude and demeanor. In typical fashion Montgomery responded to the accolades briefly and humbly, stating, "I thank ACU for preparing me for the ups and downs of life."[26] Montgomery's mother, Gladys, his grandfather Andrew Williams, and his brothers, including Cleotha and Willie, attended the dinner. His family stayed over in Irving to watch the Eagles whip the Cowboys, 31–21. Motivated by the award from ACU and especially his family's presence, Wilbert had an exceptional game, rushing for 127 yards on twenty-five carries and eclipsing the 1,000-yard mark for the second straight year. Significantly, the victory over the Cowboys rejuvenated the Eagles and put them back in the win column.[27]

After the overwhelming victory in Texas Stadium, the Eagles proceeded to win four of their last five games. Wilbert finished the regular season with 1,512 rushing yards, the best of his professional career, landing him again on the NFC All-Pro Team. Most importantly, the Eagles earned their second consecutive playoff berth. The previous year the Eagles lost in the first round, but 1979 proved to be different. The Eagles moved past their initial opponent, the Chicago Bears, 27–17, as Wilbert Montgomery outrushed Walter Payton by 20 yards. Montgomery had 87 yards on twenty-six carries while Payton ran for 67 on sixteen rushes. The Eagles, however, lost in the second round of the playoffs to the Tampa Bay Buccaneers, 24–17, when former University of Southern California star Ricky Bell ripped through Philadelphia's defense for 142 yards and two scores. The Buccaneer defense limited Montgomery to 35 yards on thirteen carries.

In 1980 sports writer Neil Warner named Wilbert Montgomery to the *Pro Football Weekly* Dream Team, a squad celebrating the rise of superstars who were selected in the late rounds of the NFL draft. Warner observed that even though Montgomery went undrafted until the sixth round in 1977, he "proved the doubters wrong" by leading the league in kickoff-return average as a rookie, by gaining 1,220 yards as an Eagles running back in 1978, and by increasing his yardage to 1,512 in 1979.[28] In the advent of the 1980 season, the same magazine called Montgomery the "best cutback runner in football. He has as much innate running ability and desire as anyone in the league, but he's an inconsistent catcher and mediocre blocker who tends to fumble."[29]

The 1980 Philadelphia Eagles had their best season during the Dick Vermeil regime. Because of injuries and defensive schemes targeting him, Wilbert Montgomery churned out only 778 yards during the regular season, yet he helped lead Philadelphia to their first ever Super Bowl appearance. The high-flying Eagles kicked off the 1980 season with three straight wins, whipping the Denver Broncos, 27–6, the Minnesota Vikings, 42–7, and the New York Giants, 35–3. Before 75,000 home fans and a Monday Night Football audience, Eagle quarterback Ron Jaworski tossed three touchdowns, while "Wil the Thrill" ran for two more to down the Giants.[30]

The Eagles' first loss of the 1980 campaign came against the St. Louis Cardinals, 24–14. The Eagles subsequently went on an eight-game winning streak before losing back-to-back games against the San Diego Chargers and the Atlanta Falcons. The Eagles defeated the Cardinals, 17–3, but lost their final regular season game to the Dallas Cowboys, 35–27. The Cowboys won the battle, but the Eagles took the war—namely, the NFC Eastern Division title.[31]

In spite of being hampered by injuries throughout the regular season, Wilbert Montgomery bounced back in a major way during the Eagles' playoff run. The Philadelphia defense forced eight turnovers as they beat Minnesota, 31–16. Like a yo-yo operating out of Philadelphia's backfield, Montgomery limped off the field repeatedly only to return and plow through the Vikings' defense. "I hurt my thigh on the first series," explained Montgomery. "Then I thought I had a concussion in the second half. Everything was blurry for awhile. Then I banged up my knee late." Testifying to his own toughness and dedication, he added, "Thigh, head, knee. Just another game. Hey, a game like this, it's a one-shot thing. I have the offseason to heal."[32]

Fresh off their convincing win, the Eagles, knowing they were but one step away from Super Bowl XV, prepared for their conference title game against arch rival Dallas Cowboys. During the regular season, the Eagles and Cowboys split their two games, each winning at home.[33] Wilbert Montgomery and his stout offensive line, however, made the difference in the drive to the Super Bowl. Running on a damaged knee before 70,696 enthused fans in freezing weather, Montgomery scorched the Cowboy defense with 194 yards and willed his team to a 20–7 victory. A determined

Montgomery acknowledged that the injury "was there, but I didn't think about it."[34] More importantly, the Eagles were Super Bowl bound for the first time in their history.

Philadelphia entered Super Bowl XV a three-point favorite over the Oakland Raiders. Since the Eagles were playing on artificial turf, had an explosive running back in Wilbert Montgomery, and had already defeated the Raiders, 10–3, earlier in the season, sports analysts gave the Eagles the advantage. The Eagles were the "walking wounded," but they had confidence.[35] Notwithstanding the sports writers' prognostications, the Raiders boasted a group of veterans, a team of "castoffs," such as Bob Chandler, Ted Hendricks, Art Shell, Gene Upshaw, and Jim Plunkett, "who know how to play football and play it so very well."[36]

Prognosticators can predict final scores and sports writers can surmise about athletes' performances, but the contest takes place on the field. In the game's first quarter, the Oakland Raiders jumped out to a 14–0 lead behind the sharp passing of veteran quarterback Jim Plunkett. A former Heisman Trophy winner from Stanford University and a ten-year NFL veteran, Plunkett hit receiver Cliff Branch for a 2-yard touchdown pass and shortly thereafter connected with running back Kenny King on an 80-yard scoring play.[37] The Raiders never looked back, holding on for a 27–10 victory over the Eagles. Oakland's defense corralled Wilbert Montgomery, limiting him to 44 yards on sixteen carries.

When asked about the Eagles' defeat, Montgomery explained, "All year we were a second-half ballclub. Today, it was like we gave up. It was a terrible feeling." Even though they entered the contest with confidence, Montgomery suggested that they lost it early in the first quarter: "I think when we failed to capitalize on a long drive early, everybody dropped their heads. We couldn't seem to get together on the sidelines. We weren't jovial. We were tense." Montgomery's own confidence failed to spill over to his teammates. "I was loose," he added. "I was confident. I just wish I could have got the other guys psyched up like I was."[38]

In spite of the agonizing loss to the Oakland Raiders in Super Bowl XV, Dick Vermeil and the Philadelphia Eagles entered the 1981 season with higher expectations than in previous years. Convinced that his team still desired to "get better," Vermeil observed, "Barring injuries I can see us being very competitive for 16 weeks (regular season schedule), but it doesn't mean we're going to win the division. I think our division will be tougher."[39] Challenged by their head coach to surpass the previous year's record, the 1981 Eagles started off 6–0 before suffering their first loss of the season to the Minnesota Vikings, 35–23. Despite the defeat, Wilbert Montgomery contributed substantially, compiling 205 all-purpose yards, 62 on the ground and 143 receiving.

The 1981 Eagles failed, however, to repeat as NFC champions, losing four out of their last five regular season games. The New York Giants took revenge against the Eagles, 20–10, and the Miami Dolphins limited Montgomery to 55 yards in a 13–10 win. The Washington Redskins then upset the Eagles, 15–13, despite Montgomery's impressive 116 rushing yards, before the Eagles snapped their four-game losing streak by shutting out St. Louis, 38–0. Coach Vermeil attributed the Eagles' four-game losing streak to "getting away from the basics." "We threw the ball a little bit more and it wasn't as productive on a consistent basis as I had hoped it would be," he explained. "We went into the St. Louis game doing what we wanted to do, and we do best, giving the ball to Montgomery."[40] Vermeil clearly understood that Wilbert Montgomery held the key to the Eagles' offensive efficiency.

The Eagles finished the 1981 regular season with a disappointing 10–6 record, putting them second in the NFC behind the 12–4 Dallas Cowboys, and prepared to host the New York Giants in the first round of the playoffs. The Eagles had soundly defeated the Giants in their opening regular season game, 24–10, but the Giants had evened the score in November, 20–10, when Montgomery had left the game three times because of injuries. He ran for 102 yards on twenty-five carries, but complained that the Giants' defense played "dirty football"—their defenders held Montgomery straight up so that two or three more could pile on.[41] Giants defenders proved to be more difficult in the postseason, limiting Montgomery to sixteen yards on eighteen carries and knocking off the Eagles, 27–17, ending their 1981 season. Even though Philadelphia lost in the first round of the playoffs, Wilbert Montgomery amassed more than 1,900 total yards—1,402 rushing and 521 receiving—during the season.

A few months after the season's end, ACU officials again honored their former star by hosting Wilbert Montgomery Day in Abilene. Garvin Beauchamp, president of the Wildcat Club, helped organize a special dinner to retire Montgomery's jersey and to establish an endowed scholarship in his name. The event featured Wilbert's high school coach Gary Dempsey, former ACU teammate Johnny Perkins, his brother Cleotha,

Angelo State's coach Jim Hess, Philadelphia Eagles teammate Bill Bergey, and Dallas Cowboys quarterback Roger Staubach. Perkins, then a receiver with the New York Giants, reflected on the 1977 NFL draft when Wilbert questioned his own ability to play professional football. "I told him he was going to be one of the best," Perkins recalled, "if not the best running back in football." Hess drew laughter from the audience when he began his remarks, stating, "I can't think of anything good to say about Wilbert Montgomery." Hess and his Rams' defense failed to stop Montgomery in the four games they played against Montgomery, going 0–3–1. Staubach called Montgomery one of the "premier" running backs in the NFL, comparing him to Gale Sayers. Such lavish comments and high praise thrilled Wilbert and brought him close to tears, especially since he greatly admired Sayers.[42]

After the 1981 season, Montgomery's numbers and the Eagles' success plummeted. The 1982 NFL strike decreased the number of regular season games from sixteen to nine. Montgomery produced 515 rushing yards and 258 receiving yards, yet the Eagles finished the season 3–6. To compound matters, head coach Dick Vermeil retired because of personal "burnout." A severe knee injury in 1983 sidelined Montgomery for most of the season, but the following year he made a comeback, piling up 1,290 all-purpose yards, 789 rushing and 501 receiving. In 1985 the Eagles traded Montgomery to the Detroit Lions, with whom he finished out his professional career backing up promising young running back Billy Sims. "This is Billy Sims' town," acknowledged Montgomery after the trade. "I know that. I know people may be looking for me to replace Billy. But nobody replaces a guy like Billy Sims."[43]

During the 1985 season Montgomery, before tearing a knee ligament, generated only 251 yards for the Lions. The following spring, Montgomery announced his retirement from the NFL, lamenting, "You can't play forever. . . . You have to know when it's time to come out of the ballgame. I can walk now. If I decided to play another year, maybe something severe will happen to me."[44]

Wilbert Montgomery exited the NFL the same way he entered: without fanfare. He limped away with no rushing title or championship ring, but he had gained nearly 7,000 yards on the ground and had led his team to their first Super Bowl appearance. Along the way, however, he had paid a heavy price and bore the scars to prove it. Sports writer Bill Lyon, indicting the Philadelphia Eagles for wringing Montgomery "dry" only to discard him as "used tissue," assessed,

> In the glory years of Dick Vermeil, Montgomery was the Eagles' offensive hoss, and they rode him and rode him and rode him. They rode him hard, and they put him up wet. He would take the pitchback and then sweep wide, always accelerating, burrowing gamely ahead, head down, even when there was no hole.[45]

After being drafted in the sixth round by the Philadelphia Eagles, Wilbert Montgomery simply wanted to make the team. And he did, but he accomplished much more. He never clamored for praise and recognition about individual achievements. Eagles general manager Jim Murray once observed that King Tut might be a better interview than Wilbert Montgomery, adding: "He's Whispering Wilbert. He talks with his feet. The other guys have the good quotes; he has the yardage."[46] When Montgomery retired from football, he was—and remains today—the Eagles' all-time leading rusher, with 6,789 yards and forty-five touchdowns. Just as he had done in Abilene, Texas, Montgomery left an indelible mark on Eagles followers. Contemporary fans, regrettably, may know little about Wilbert Montgomery and his remarkable feats, but the self-effacing running back would want to keep it that way.

Chapter 9

From Player to Mentor: Wilbert Montgomery as a Running Backs Coach in the NFL

As iron sharpeneth iron, so one sharpens another.

Proverbs 27:17

After walking away from the National Football League in 1985, Wilbert Montgomery poured himself into multiple projects—working as a salesman for Rich Paper Company in New Jersey, hosting a talk radio show, and partnering with other former professional athletes such as Ron Jaworski and Carl Peterson to establish sporting goods stores. Of those various endeavors, Montgomery most enjoyed working on the talk radio show *Around the Football League*, which he hosted for eight years, inviting former and current NFL players to discuss issues dealing with professional football. Additionally, when the Philadelphia Eagles hired Ray Rhodes, a Texas native and former player, to be their head coach in 1995, Rhodes offered Montgomery a position, but he declined because his off-the-field ventures proved to be more lucrative.[1]

On August 17, 1996, a decade after his retirement from the National Football League, Wilbert Montgomery resurfaced on national sports pages with his induction into the College Football Hall of Fame in South

Wilbert Montgomery standing between his former professional coach Dick Vermeil (*left*) and his former collegiate coach Wally Bullington (*right*) at the College Football Hall of Fame in South Bend, Indiana, 1996. Courtesy of Abilene Christian University.

Bend, Indiana. Those joining him as members of the class of 1996 included former Louisiana Tech quarterback Terry Bradshaw, Jackson State running back Walter Payton, defensive tackle Buck Buchanan from Grambling State, quarterback Neil Lomax who played for Portland State, Widener University alum receiver Billy "White Shoes" Johnson, and former Northwestern State linebacker Gary Reasons.

Wilbert Montgomery, the press release noted, finished his Abilene Christian University (ACU) career with 3,047 rushing yards and led the Wildcats to a 33–10–1 record during his four years' tenure. In the process he scored thirty-one touchdowns in 1973, adding thirty-nine more during his four years at ACU. A couple of months later Wilbert Montgomery became the first athlete selected for ACU's affiliated league's Lone Star Conference Hall of Honor. The Hall also inducted three former conference officials, along with football coach Gil Steinke of Texas A&M–Kingsville, basketball coach Phil George of Angelo State, and athletic director Dr. Jess Hawthorne of Texas A&M–Commerce.[2] Some eleven years after his remarkable gridiron exploits, Montgomery might well bask in such recognition, but these signal honors, the highest a player can receive, did not mark his end with football.

The next year Dick Vermeil returned to the NFL as head coach of the St. Louis Rams and hired Wilbert Montgomery as his running backs coach. Indeed, Vermeil also brought over other former players and staff members from the Philadelphia Eagles to help him lead the Rams. He appointed John Bunting as the team's linebackers coach. He then hired Carl Hairston to coach the defensive line, Dick Coury to tutor wide receivers, Jerry Rhome to serve as offensive coordinator, and Lem Burnham to fill the role of team psychologist. Vermeil trusted these men, having worked with them previously, and he also saw this as a "way of paying" a "debt."[3]

Since Wilbert Montgomery lacked previous coaching experience, Vermeil assigned special teams coach Frank Gansz to help him catch on. Having coached Montgomery for five years when he was with the Eagles, Vermeil knew his former running back's commitment and dedication to the game, and he never forgot his toughness and work ethic. "I told Wilbert when I left Philadelphia, if I had a major corporation he would be my vice president," Vermeil said. "Nobody ever gave more to the game for me as a head coach than Wilbert. I never coached a superstar that worked harder on the practice field than that guy did."[4]

In spite of his earlier success with the Eagles, leading the St. Louis Rams to the top of the NFL proved no easy task. In 1996 the Rams chose Lawrence Phillips as their number one draft pick, a talented yet troubled running back out of the University of Nebraska. In college Phillips, in a jealous rage, climbed a wall to reach his former girlfriend's apartment, found her hiding in a bathroom, and dragged her by her hair down three flights of stairs. Phillips pleaded guilty to trespassing and assault and received a probation sentence; the Cornhuskers then suspended Phillips for six games, which likely cost him the Heisman Trophy in 1995. Despite such glaring character flaws the St. Louis Rams, under the direction of head coach Rich Brooks, made Phillips the sixth overall pick and their number-one choice in the 1996 NFL draft.[5]

Dick Vermeil assumed leadership of the St. Louis Rams in 1997 and admitted, "I probably wouldn't have drafted him [Phillips]. And I told

Wilbert Montgomery standing outside of the College Football Hall of Fame in South Bend, Indiana, where he was inducted in 1996. Courtesy of Abilene Christian University.

Lawrence that." Yet Vermeil believed that Phillips was not beyond repair. "I'm glad I have him—not only because he's a talented guy, but because he's on our roster and he's one of our team members. Plus, I like these kinds of projects." Vermeil especially hoped that Wilbert Montgomery could help mold Phillips's work ethic and demeanor. Like Vermeil, Montgomery knew that Phillips had great potential and he hoped that his protégé could be reformed and redeemed. "As a physical specimen, Lawrence Phillips could be one of the great runners in the NFL," Montgomery stated. "He reminds me of Marcus Allen with those long, loping strides and bunny-hop style, the cutting back. He can hit right at the point of attack and get outside. And he has the size to move the pile." Knowing that he himself had received a second chance, Montgomery willingly gave Phillips the same opportunity that had proved so pivotal in his own life. Phillips "needs a

Wilbert Montgomery stands with his talented protégé, Ray Rice, before an NFL game. Courtesy of Phil Hoffmann of the Baltimore Ravens.

family," Montgomery believed, "and that's what we're trying to build with the Rams. Lawrence needs to feel a part of it."[6]

Regrettably, Phillips would not work under the leadership of the Rams' "father" or heed the ministrations of his "brother" coach, and St. Louis released him in 1997 after he got into a heated dispute with coach Vermeil over limited playing time. The Rams finished the season with a 5–11 record, and the following year they fell to an even more dismal 4–12. Following the 1998 season the Rams traded for Louisiana native Marshall Faulk. After a prolific college career at San Diego State, Faulk played four years with the Indianapolis Colts. Upon joining the Rams, Faulk became the catalyst for the so-called Greatest Show on Turf, amassing 2,429 total yards—1,381 on the ground and 1,048 receiving yards. Complementing the spectacular passing combination of Kurt Warner to Isaac Bruce and Torry Holt, Faulk led the Rams to a win over the Tennessee Titans in Super Bowl XXXIV. When asked about his mentoring of Faulk, the modest Montgomery simply called it a "pleasure to coach someone with that kind of ability."[7]

In addition to Marshall Faulk, Wilbert Montgomery also mentored Steven Jackson, a 6'2", 236-pound running back from Oregon State University, whom the Rams drafted in 2004. Jackson became Faulk's backup; and, in spite of limited playing time, he rushed for 673 on 134 carries and four touchdowns. As Faulk's health declined, Jackson became the starter, and in 2005 he tallied 1,046 yards and eight touchdowns while catching forty-three passes for 320 yards. From 2006 to 2008 Montgomery moved to the Detroit Lions as the running backs coach; he mentored Kevin Jones, a talented product from Virginia Tech who had been the thirtieth pick of the draft in 2004. Four years later, however, the Lions released Jones after a series of injuries convinced the coaching staff that he lacked durability. In 2008 the Baltimore Ravens hired Montgomery in the same capacity. In this position Montgomery again considered it a "pleasure" to work with such talented runners as Le'Ron McClain, Willis McGahee, and Ray Rice.[8] McClain recently called his running back coach "straightforward," a "great father," and a "good man." He credited Montgomery with giving him the confidence to "make it in the NFL as a running back and fullback." McGahee similarly expressed appreciation for Montgomery because of his work ethic and his being a "great family man." He also thanked Montgomery for standing up for his running backs when other "coaches are down on them." The Ravens' premier running back, Ray Rice, said that Montgomery was his "mentor" and a "fierce competitor." Knowing that his running back coach had a successful NFL career, Rice gladly ingests his instruction, soaking it up "like a sponge."[9] Montgomery learned from experience what it took to survive and thrive in professional football, testifying in a recent interview, "When I stepped on the field, I was always going to give 110 percent on every given snap."[10] Because his personal experiences and inspiring personality, Montgomery has turned out a series of exceptional, Pro Bowl–level runners.

Wilbert Montgomery has trained and continues to help develop gifted running backs for several NFL teams, leaving an indelible mark on the game of football. Many NFL fans who have cheered the feats of Marshall

Wilbert Montgomery supervises a practice session as running backs coach for the Baltimore Ravens. Courtesy of Phil Hoffmann of the Baltimore Ravens.

Faulk, Steven Jackson, Kevin Jones, Le'Ron McClain, Willis McGahee, and Ray Rice may not see the hand of a veteran athlete from the Mississippi Delta who played his collegiate football at a small, predominantly white college in West Texas.

His fellow NFL coaches, however, have understood and valued Montgomery's growing expertise. Recently, Minnesota Vikings running backs coach Eric Bieniemy asked Wilbert Montgomery for help in teaching his backs how to hang on to the football. Bieniemy has been troubled by the chronic fumbling of his talented protégé, Adrian Peterson. Montgomery advised Bieniemy to get fifteen-pound footballs and put stockings over them. The weighted footballs with stockings would make the balls heavy and slippery, forcing running backs to focus on keeping the ball tightly gripped.[11] Montgomery himself had fumbled the football at crucial times in his own career, so he brought a personal perspective to the problem.

Dick Vermeil launched the inexperienced Montgomery's coaching career because of his own recollections of his drive and determination. He
gave the former Philadelphia Eagles star a shot at coaching at the professional level, convinced that Montgomery would bring a full and fierce
commitment to the task of coaching NFL running backs. In Vermeil's
opinion, the untried Montgomery remained peerless. Even though Vermeil and Montgomery failed to win a Super Bowl championship as coach
and player with the Philadelphia Eagles, they succeeded as fellow coaches
for the Rams. The same "thrill" Montgomery brought to Vermeil and the
Eagles as a player, he experienced himself when he mentored the Rams'
Marshall Faulk and Steven Jackson, the Detroit Lions' Kevin Jones, and
then the Ravens' Le'Ron McClain, Willis McGahee, and Ray Rice, instill-
ing in them the determined drive imperative for any successful NFL runner. Montgomery's success as a professional coach sprang from the same
combination of physical skills and mental toughness that propelled him to
the top as a player. And he has shown the rare ability to inspirit others with
this same indomitable spirit.

Epilogue: The Legacy of Wilbert Montgomery

I wasn't cocky when I came to the Bears, but I knew I could play.

Gale Sayers (quoted in Richard Whittingham, *What Bears They Were*, 15)

He's [Wilbert Montgomery] the best ball carrier I've ever seen. I used to think Warren McVea was the best, but Wilbert is bigger and maybe faster.

Chuck Moser, legendary Texas football coach (quoted in Mark McDonald, "Odds Against ACC Repeat," *Abilene Reporter News*, September 1, 1974)

Born and reared in the Mississippi Delta, Wilbert Montgomery emerged from obscurity on the campus of Abilene Christian University in West Texas. Nurtured by a mother's love and a grandfather's toughness, and disciplined by the demands of a high school coach, he went on to leave indelible marks on the game of football at both the collegiate and professional levels. Yet his achievements have almost been forgotten.

In recent years ACU's football teams have enjoyed great success, garnering national rankings and playing in national playoff games of Division II. Former ACU player and coach Bob Strader finds the seeds of this more recent success in the triumphs of an often neglected past: "The only reason we were champions was because of Wilbert Montgomery. He was a turning point in ACC athletics and ACC football." Across the years ACC had landed many prized athletes, including Olympic champions Bobby Joe Morrow, Earl Young, and Billy Olson, but they were "not like Wilbert. He was spectacular."[1]

The NFL has taken notice of ACU's talent. The Chicago Bears chose Danieal Manning (now a member of the Houston Texans) as the first pick in the second round of the 2006 draft; three years later the Bears tapped ACU's speedy receiver Johnny Knox in the fifth round. One round later the Cincinnati Bengals drafted former ACU running back Bernard Scott, winner of the 2008 Harlon Hill Trophy, the Heisman Trophy equivalent for Division II. Manning, Knox, and Scott obliterated a number of university and conference records during their careers in West Texas, perhaps helping to push Montgomery's feats farther back into the recesses of the minds of college football fans.

It appears that most African American athletes at ACU have conformed to the image of Wilbert Montgomery as an athlete-student instead of that of Paul Robeson, the scholar-baller. Like Montgomery, Danieal Manning, Johnny Knox, and Bernard Scott starred at ACU and departed without completing their degrees, apparently choosing to use college athletics as a launching pad to the NFL. Robeson conversely used the gridiron to advance his academic and political careers.[2] The careers and tenures of Montgomery, Manning, Knox, and Scott at ACU raise some questions: Did these black athletes use ACU to advance their own goals of making it to the NFL? Or did ACU exploit gifted black athletes to attract similar standout athletes to help them win more championships and gain more notoriety and a greater reputation as a national football powerhouse? Does ACU expend talented black athletes to enhance and enrich itself, or do black athletes exploit the system with an eye to playing professionally? Do ACU administrators care more about winning championships than about molding young black men into the images of Paul Robeson and Jesus Christ? The answers to these questions remain nebulous and complicated.

Even though the foregoing questions are beyond the scope of this book, one fact remains clear: Wilbert Montgomery's legacy as a collegiate and professional football player has been virtually eclipsed. Today most NFL fans, and certainly those in Pennsylvania, recall the scrambling ability of Philadelphia Eagle Randall Cunningham, who arrived just as Montgomery was leaving. Others recall Vince Papale's inspiring story, which has been dramatized in the movie *Invincible*. A schoolteacher and bar bouncer, Papale earned a spot on a special team for the Eagles. Ron Jaworski, Eagles quarterback during Montgomery's tenure, now analyzes professional football before a national audience on Monday Night Football and the ESPN sports network. And many Philadelphians still avidly follow the career of their longtime quarterback, Donovan McNabb, although he was traded by the Eagles to the hated Washington Redskins. The stream of praise and accolades showered upon these quality players has perhaps consigned Montgomery's fascinating tale to obscurity.

Yet before he could strap on his football gear, Montgomery had to cope with a West Texas culture where long-segregated blacks had yet to find their level of comfort and contribution. So the youthful black athlete from the Mississippi Delta showed up on a freshly integrated West Texas Christian college campus, and perhaps unwittingly helped improve race relations to that point that blacks and whites were just learning to trust and even love one another. White Christians at ACU, especially the Dick Felts family, quickly befriended Wilbert, becoming his surrogate family. Such encounters taught the reticent and inexperienced young man to trust white people, and to extend his love to those outside his race. The ACU environment so impressed Montgomery that he swayed a number of outstanding black student-athletes from the Mississippi Delta to enroll at ACU. ACU changed Wilbert Montgomery, but he also changed the university and the community around it.

Montgomery swiftly emerged on the national collegiate football scene with a stunning freshman year performance, shattering long-held national marks. Perhaps the most remarkable feat remains his amazing tally of seventy-six touchdowns; in the storied history of college football, no player had ever scored more in a career. Montgomery also capped off his freshman year by leading his team to a national championship. Yet apart from his football triumphs, Montgomery dealt with the difficulties of playing and schooling in a traditionally white environment. Although he encountered an occasional rough patch, he moved effectively in the West Texas university and community, bringing along the mostly white fans in the area who came to appreciate Montgomery's accomplishments and to understand how little his skin color mattered. In the process he learned how to function successfully but without compromise in a largely white world, aided by a university community that had learned to take its Christian commitments seriously. Underscoring the validity and opportunities inherent in this kind of growth, which he had undergone and led, was Montgomery's successful effort to bring a number of black Mississippi athletes to Abilene and ACU, a community and school that grew along with these southern recruits.

In a football-mad region such as West Texas, the impact of a black, extraordinarily talented athlete gaining national renown can easily be underestimated. Young boys growing up wanting to be like Wilbert paid no attention to his skin color. And as such boys grew into manhood, they carried with them a certain disregard for racial differences. It is no easy thing to shift long-held racial perceptions, but it cannot be doubted that Wilbert Montgomery contributed importantly to this transition in West Texas. At the same time he helped forward his own football career ambitions.

Upon entering the world of professional football, where by the 1970s yardage gain more often than not trumped race, Montgomery brought with him the strategies of coping with racism that he had learned in Abilene. Although he played in an integrated city, he on occasion faced the vituperation of racist fans and handled such situations with dispatch. On the field, he came under the tutelage of head coach Dick Vermeil, who grasped just how important a runner like Montgomery could be. Effectively using and building upon his collegiate experiences while learning the nuances of the professional game, Montgomery led the Philadelphia Eagles to their first-ever Super Bowl. Unfortunately, as is true of many running backs, the rigors of the game shortened his career; injuries took their implacable toll. Still Montgomery's ties with coach Vermeil were severed only temporarily.

Nine years after Montgomery stepped away from the field, Dick Vermeil took the reins of the St. Louis Rams and immediately tapped him to coach the Rams running backs. It appeared an unusual choice since Montgomery had no coaching experience, but Vermeil understood the dedication, drive, and football intelligence of his former Eagles star and was convinced he could transmit this to his charges in St. Louis. Once again, Montgomery proved faithful to his calling; the Rams won Super Bowl XXXIV, with the Montgomery-coached Marshall Faulk leading the ground game and winning the NFL Offensive Player of the Year award. This was Montgomery's first coaching stop, and other successful ones have followed for more than a decade. He has proven an usually effective mentor for the ball carriers under his tutelage; wherever he has coached, his runners have set records.

Owner of more than a few such marks himself, Wilbert Montgomery gained his experience when the on-field obstacles sometimes paled before those faced in the more fiercely racist society of previous decades. Yet the unprepossessing black youth from Mississippi not only passed through these troubled waters effectively, but also left behind a coterie of friends and fans—from Mississippi to West Texas to Philadelphia and beyond—who came to appreciate and admire his athletic talents and quiet demeanor on the field and off.

Wilbert Montgomery surely changed ACU, but ACU also changed Montgomery, making him a better person and a better athlete. Montgomery has picked up the challenge of transforming lives as he has mentored young, talented athletes in the National Football League with the St. Louis Rams, the Detroit Lions, and now the Baltimore Ravens. Those who saw him play for the ACU Wildcats have never forgotten his "unreal" moves on the football field, and the Lone Star Conference Hall of Fame remembered by tapping Montgomery in 1996. In addition, the College Football Hall of Fame remembered Montgomery and inducted him into the class of 1996. Should professional football also bestow on Wilbert Montgomery its highest honor by electing him to its Hall of Fame, the circle could be closed—completing a story important for any who seek to understand the role of sports and sportsmen in contemporary American society.

The Pro Football Hall of Fame has already bestowed the highest honor on a few African American athletes from the Lone Star Conference. Darrell Green, a native of Houston, became standout defensive back and track star at Texas A&I (now Texas A&M University) at Kingsville. After being drafted in the first round in 1983 by the Washington Redskins, Green played almost two decades with the Washington Redskins, garnered seven Pro Bowl selections, won two Super Bowl rings, and in 2008 received enshrinement in the National Football Hall of Fame.[3]

Two years later, the Pro Football Hall of Fame enshrined John Randle, another former exceptional athlete from the Lone Star Conference. A native of Mumford, Texas, Randle played junior college football at Trinity Valley Community College in Athens, Texas, before starring two years for the Javelinas in Kingsville. Unlike Green, who was drafted in the first round, Randle in 1990 signed on with the Minnesota Vikings as an undrafted free agent. Despite being considered too small by most teams, Randle went on to play thirteen years in the National Football League—ten with the Vikings and three with the Seattle Seahawks. Even though

Randle never won a Super Bowl ring, he made the Pro Bowl team seven times. Wilbert Montgomery hailed from the same conference as did Green and Randle, but he has yet to receive the same lofty honor given by the Professional Football Hall of Fame. Even though Montgomery never won two Super Bowl rings and did not make the Pro Bowl team seven times, Montgomery is still deserving of enshrinement in Canton, Ohio. In 1999 Montgomery won a Super Bowl ring as a running backs coach with the St. Louis Rams, while mentoring 2011 Hall of Famer inductee Marshall Faulk. Moreover, Montgomery continues to contribute to the game by coaching and guiding other promising running backs in the National Football League.

In addition, the Pro Football Hall of Fame elected Floyd Little to the class of 2010. Little, a three-time All-America running back from Syracuse University, became the Denver Broncos' first pick in 1967. When Little left the game in 1973, he was the seventh leading rusher—with 6,323 yards and fifty-four touchdowns. By the time Little retired from the professional game, Wilbert Montgomery had emerged as a collegiate gridiron star about to soar with the Philadelphia Eagles. When Montgomery left the National Football League in 1985, he had amassed more rushing yards—6,789 and fifty-seven touchdowns—than Little. The former also amassed more receiving yards than the latter; Montgomery ended his career with 2,502 receiving yards to Little's 2,418.[4] Montgomery accomplished his feats as the professional game was becoming more complicated and more sophisticated.[5] If Little, who ended his career with fewer rushing and receiving yards than Montgomery and who never earned a Super Bowl ring as a player, recently received enshrinement in Canton, why deny Montgomery this honor?

Before quarterback Ron Jaworski transitioned from the Los Angeles Rams to the Philadelphia Eagles in 1977, he was known for being a "boastful" and "excitable" player who gave a lot of "lively quotes." Jaworski once quipped, "There's a spot reserved for me in the Hall of Fame."[6] Although Jaworski issued that statement to generate controversy in the Rams' locker-room, the declaration certainly applies more accurately to his former Philadelphia Eagles teammate. Hopefully there remains a "spot reserved" in the National Football League's Hall of Fame for Wilbert Montgomery.

Appendix I

Wilbert Montgomery's Collegiate Statistics

1973: 11–1 (Freshman Season)

	Versus	TC	RuYds	PC	ReYds	TDs
Game 1:	Arkansas State	2	6	3	55	2
Game 2:	Texas A&I	16	77	2	9	2
Game 3:	SWTSU	8	5	5	119	4
Game 4:	SFA	17	146	9	174	6
Game 5:	ETSU	8	50	1	-3	1
Game 6:	Sul Ross (Home-coming)	***Did not play—injured				
Game 7:	Angelo State	22	165	1	8	3
Game 8:	Tarleton St.	21	168	4	35	4
Game 9:	Sam Houston	16	109	2	49	5
Game 10:	Howard Payne	26	127	3	65	4

REGULAR SEASON TOTALS:		136	854	30	411	31
Game 11:	Langston Univ.	24	168	2	7	4
Game 12:	Elon Univ.	21	159	4	79	2
POSTSEASON TOTALS:		45	327	6	86	6

*TC=Total Carries
*RuYds=Rushing Yards
*PC=Pass Catches
*ReYds=Receiving Yards
*TDs=Touchdowns

Compiled from *The Wilbert Montgomery File* at Abilene Christian University.

Appendix II

Wilbert Montgomery's Collegiate Statistics

1974: 7–4 (Sophomore Season)

	Versus	TC	RuYds	PC	ReYds	TDs
Game 1:	State College of AR:	20	47	2	24	4
Game 2:	Nebras-ka–Omaha	17	109	3	105	3
Game 3:	Texas A&I	12	40	3	23	1
Game 4:	SWTSU	19	101	1	-2	3
Game 5:	SFA	26	95	1	-9	1
Game 6:	ETSU	23	102	1	-3	2
Game 7:	Sul Ross (Home-coming)	***Did not play—injured				
Game 8:	Angelo State	6	69	0	0	1
Game 9:	Tarleton State	***Did not play—injured				

Game 10:	SHSU	***Did not play—injured				
Game 11:	Howard Payne	20	94	0	0	2
REGULAR SEASON TOTALS:		143	657	11	138	17

*TC=Total Carries
*Ru Yds=Rushing Yards
*PC=Pass Catches
*ReYds=Receiving Yards
*TDs=Touchdowns

Compiled from *The Wilbert Montgomery File* at Abilene Christian University.

Appendix III

Wilbert Montgomery's Collegiate Statistics

1975: 6–3–1 (Junior Season)

	Versus	TC	RuYds	PC	ReYds	TDs
Game 1:	Troy State	14	101	3	42	3
Game 2:	Texas A&I	5	32	1	-6	1
Game 3:	SWTSU	16	87	4	22	2
Game 4:	SFA	5	36	1	25	1
Game 5:	ETSU	***Did not play—injured				
Game 6:	Sul Ross (Home-coming)	***Did not play—injured				
Game 7:	Angelo State	6	22	0	0	0
Game 8:	Tarleton St.	27	213	2	32	2
Game 9:	SHSU	10	60	0	0	3
Game 10:	Howard Payne	21	61	2	12	2
REGULAR SEASON TOTALS:		114	612	13	127	14

*TC=Total Carries
*RuYds=Rushing Yards
*PC=Pass Catches
*ReYds=Receiving Yards
*TDs=Touchdowns

Compiled from *The Wilbert Montgomery File* at Abilene Christian University.

Appendix IV

Wilbert Montgomery's Collegiate Statistics

1976: 9–2 (Senior Season)

	Versus	TC	RuYds	PC	ReYds	TDs
Game 1:	North West OK	9	31	2	65	2
Game 2:	Northern CO	13	50	4	8	0
Game 3:	Texas A&I	24	80	0	0	0
Game 4:	SWTSU	14	45	5	38	1
Game 5:	SFA	10	137	1	16	1
Game 6:	ETSU	(HC)	21	120	1	43
Game 7:	Angelo State	11	35	8	135	2
Game 8:	Cameron Univ.	6	99	1	3	1
Game 9:	SHSU	***Did not play—injured				
Game 10:	Howard Payne	***Did not play—injured				

REGULAR SEASON TOTALS:	108	597	22	308	8
POST-SEASON GAME:	***Did not play—injured				

*TC=Total Carries
*RuYds=Rushing Yards
*PC=Pass Catches
*ReYds=Receiving Yards
*TDs=Touchdowns
*HC=Homecoming

Compiled from *The Wilbert Montgomery File* at Abilene Christian University.

Appendix V

Wilbert Montgomery's NFL Statistics

	TC	RuYds	PC	ReYds	TDs
PHI (1977):	45	183	3	18	2
PHI (1978):	259	1220	34	195	10
PHI (1979):	338	1512	41	494	14
PHI (1980):	193	778	50	407	10
PHI (1981):	286	1402	49	521	10
PHI (1982):	114	515	20	258	9
PHI (1983):	29	139	9	53	0
PHI (1984):	201	789	60	501	2
DET (1985):	75	251	7	55	0
NFL TOTALS:	1,540	6,789	273	2,502	57

*TC=Total Carries
*RuYds=Rushing Yards
*PC=Pass Catches
*ReYds=Receiving Yards
*TDs=Touchdowns

Adapted from Sean Lahman, *The Pro Football Historical Abstract*, 419.

Notes

Prologue

1. Mark McDonald, "Call Him Mr. Touchdown," *Texas Football Newsmagazine,* January–February 1974, 21. The flat pass to Wilbert Montgomery was called "fake 31 draw, slip to the 2 back at 8." See Mark McDonald, "ACC 'Flying' on Fast Feet of Montgomery," *Abilene Reporter News,* October 2, 1973, 1-C.
2. Hubert Pickett, interview by Edward J. Robinson, March 12, 2010.
3. George Breazeale, "ACC's National Champs Lone Star's Best Ever?" *Texas Football Newsmagazine,* January–February 1974, 21. Gilbert Steinke (1919–1995) and his Javelinas from Kingsville were a thorn in the side of ACC and other LSC athletic foes. A native of Brenham, Texas, a former Javelina football star, and former professional football player, Steinke coached the Texas A&I (now Texas A&M University at Kingsville) Javelinas for twenty-three years, from 1954 to 1976. He won six National Athletic Intercollegiate Association (NAIA) championships and compiled an impressive 182–61–2 record. From 1974 to 1976, his Javelinas put together three consecutive undefeated teams. This information was abstracted from "The National Football Foundation and College Hall of Fame, Inc." (Larchmont, NY: 1996), 30, in the *Wilbert Montgomery File* at Abilene Christian University. Steinke's comment about Montgomery mirrored that of Vince Dooley, head coach of the Georgia Bulldogs, who prepared to stop Jerry LeVias and the SMU Mustangs in the 1966 Cotton Bowl. Dooley, raving about Jerry LeVias's ability, stated, "LeVias jumps like a kangaroo and runs like a jackrabbit" (quoted in Pennington, *Breaking the Ice,* 99).
4. For a thorough discussion of the debate of so-called "black athletic superiority," see chapter 9 in Wiggins, *Glory Bound,* 177–99.

5. Wiggins, "Great Speed But Little Stamina," 162–64, 166–67.

6. Wiggins, "Great Speed But Little Stamina," 168–69. See also Carroll, *Red Grange and the Rise of Modern Football,* 35; Dyreson, "American Ideas about Race and Olympic Races," 173–215.

7. Quoted in Pennington, *Breaking the Ice,* 43.

8. Jerry LeVias quoted in Pennington, *Breaking the Ice,* 100. For Wilbert Montgomery's comment, see Bill Hart, "Defense Wins Bet, ACC Shell A&I with Offense," *Abilene Reporter News,* September 23, 1973, 1. See also Wiggins, "Great Speed But Little Stamina," 185.

9. Quoted in Pennington, *Breaking the Ice,* 154.

10. Fitzpatrick, *And the Walls Came Tumbling Down,* 6, 28.

11. Rhoden, *Forty Million Dollar Slaves,* 129.

12. Demas, "Integrating the Gridiron," 6, 29.

13. Graham and Cody, *Getting Open.*

14. Pennington, *Breaking the Ice,* 8–9.

15. Katherine Lopez, *Cougars of Any Color,* 170.

16. Pennington, *Breaking the Ice,* 50, 84, 122.

17. Colter Hettich, "First African-American Student Recalls Struggle," *Optimist,* May 1, 2009, 5. See also Hughes, *Reviving the Ancient Faith,* 289–90. On the role black preachers in Churches of Christ played in contesting the racism in white Church of Christ colleges, see Robinson, *The Fight Is On in Texas.*

18. Brandon Tripp, "Breaking the ACU Color Barrier: Integration of ACU Sports Promotes Stronger Teams, Peaceful Community," *Optimist,* May 1, 2009, 11.

19. Pennington, *Breaking the Ice,* 12. For the forgotten story of Pete Pedro, see Joyce Erekson, "Pete Pedro Honored at West Texas A&M University," *Daily Item of Lynn,* October 18, 2010, accessed December 6, 2010, www.dailyitemoflynn.com.

20. Stevens, *No Ordinary University.*

21. Eig, *Opening Day,* 275. Most sports historians recognize that Jackie Robinson was not the first African American to play major league baseball. In the mid-1880s, Moses Fleetwood Walker (1857–1924), an African American baseball player at Oberlin College and the University of Michigan, played professional baseball for Toledo in the Northwestern League (Zang, *Fleet Walker's Divided Heart,* 24; Shropshire, *In Black and White*).

I am aware that some sports historians view the legacy of Jackie Robinson pejoratively. John Hoberman insists that the contention that Jackie Robinson's entry into professional baseball to complete integration of American society is a myth (*Darwin's Athletes,* 31). See also Brower, "The Black Side of Football," 12–16. Brower observes that in 1946 Kenny Washington, a member of the Los Angeles Rams, became the first African American player in the NFL six months before Jackie Robinson reintegrated major league baseball (55). See also Ross, *Outside the Lines,* 82, 88–90.

22. Hirsch, *Willie Mays,* 159, 227.

23. Morris, *The Courting of Marcus Dupree* (New York: Doubleday, 1983), 177 (Marty Stuart quotation), 183 (Cella Conner quotation).

24. John C. Whitley, interview by Edward J. Robinson, June 29, 2010; Bob Strader, interview by Edward J. Robinson, July 21, 2010.

Chapter 1

1. Bullard, *Free at Last,* 17.

2. Branch, *Parting the Waters,* 25, 112–113; McMillen, *The Citizens' Council.*

3. Cobb, *The Most Southern Place on Earth.*

4. Cobb, *The Most Southern Place on Earth,* 183.

5. Charles S. Johnson, *Growing Up in the Black Belt,* 30.

6. Bullard, *Free at Last,* 40–45, 54, 60–61, 70–73. See also Hudson-Weems, *Emmett Till.* For other more recent and insightful studies on the racial climate of the Mississippi Delta, see Tisdale, "Medgar Evers"; Moye, "Sick and Tired of Being Sick and Tired," 8, 27; Lee, *For Freedom's Sake;* Wood, "The Roots of Black Power"; Gillespie, "They Walk, Talk, and Act Like New People." For examples of the stark segregation that pervaded the Magnolia State, see Perkins, *Let Justice Roll Down,* 88. Perkins, a native Mississippian, has observed that the state of Mississippi paid $4.4 million to transport white children to school and $1.1 million to transport black children to school. State officials expended $23.5 million to instruct white children, in contrast to $8.8 million to educate black children. Mississippi paid white teachers an annual salary of $2,109 and black teachers an annual salary of $1,553.

7. Quoted in Cobb, *The Most Southern Place on Earth,* 117.

8. McMillen, *Dark Journey,* 262. Richard Wright's insightful observation is analyzed in Wilkerson, *The Warmth of Other Suns,* 13.

9. Art Lawler, "Honing Their Skills on the Delta," *Abilene Reporter News,* August 31, 1975, 5-F.

10. Wilbert Montgomery, interview by Edward J. Robinson, June 16, 2010.

11. Mike Freeman states that Brown, native of St. Simons Island, Georgia, was abandoned by his father when he was two weeks old (*Jim Brown,* 17).

12. Blair, *Earl Campbell,* 13.

13. "Wilbert's Deception Eagles' Gain," *Abilene Reporter News,* November 8, 1978, 1-C.

14. Mark McDonald, "ACC 'Flying' on Fast Feet of Montgomery," *Abilene Reporter News,* October 2, 1973, 1-C.

15. "Wilbert's Deception Eagles' Gain," 2-C.

16. "Wilbert's Deception Eagles' Gain," 2-C.

17. "Wilbert's Deception Eagles' Gain," 2-C.

18. Gordon Forbes, "A Quiet Man Leaves All the Talk to Others," *Philadelphia Inquirer,* March 2, 1979, 1-C.

19. Wilbert Montgomery, interview, June 16, 2010.

20. "Wilbert's Deception Eagles' Gain," 2-C.
21. "Three New Coaches Added at GHS," *Delta Democrat-Times,* September 2, 1970, 10.
22. "Frank Davis Named GHS Grid Assistant," *Delta Democrat-Times,* September 15, 1972, 15.
23. Gary Dempsey, interview by Edward J. Robinson, July 24, 2009.

Chapter 2

1. Gary Dempsey, interview by Edward J. Robinson, July 24, 2009.
2. Gary Dempsey, interview by Edward J. Robinson, July 6, 2010.
3. Mitch Ariff commented that Wilbert "proved to be a thorn in the side of Lee all night" with his "twisting runs" ("Hornets Rip Columbus Lee, 35–0, in Opener," *Delta Democrat-Times,* September 12, 1971, 10).
4. "First Full Day of Classes Goes Smoothly," *Delta Democrat-Times,* September 4, 1970, 1; and Penny Jenkins, "Majority to Minority Transfers End Oct. 1," *Delta Democrat-Times,* September 11, 1970, 14.
5. Dempsey, interview, July 6, 2010.
6. Jim Dent, "What's a Country Boy Like Wilbert Doing Super-Hype Bowl?" *Sports-Week,* January 23, 1981, 4.
7. Elliott Williams, "Letters to the Editor: 'Student Seeks Unity,'" *Delta Democrat-Times,* August 31, 1971, 4.
8. "Letters to the Editor: 'On the Wrong Track,'" *Delta Democrat-Times,* September 13, 1971, 4.
9. "Hornets Top Caldwell," *Delta Democrat-Times,* September 19, 1971, 20.
10. Mitch Ariff, "Hornets Gain Third Loop Win," *Delta Democrat-Times,* September 26, 1971, 9.
11. Mitch Ariff, "Hornets Rip Cleveland for 4th Win," *Delta Democrat-Times,* October 3, 1971, 10.
12. Mitch Ariff, "GHS Hornets Defang Meridian Wildcats," *Delta Democrat-Times,* October 10, 1971, 10.
13. Mitch Ariff, "Hornets Sting Corinth for Sixth Straight," *Delta Democrat-Times,* October 17, 1971, 10.
14. Mitch Ariff, "Hornets Sting Zebras, 34–12," *Delta Democrat-Times,* October 26, 1971, 9.
15. Mitch Ariff, "GHS Clinches Tie for North Division Title," *Delta Democrat-Times,* October 31, 1971, 19.
16. Lavonne Morris, "After the Game, Back Go the Walls," *Delta Democrat-Times,* October 31, 1971, 24.
17. Quoted in H. G. Bissinger, *Friday Night Lights,* 107. Branch, when assessing the Montgomery bus boycott, pointed out that white bus drivers enforced a "'floating line' between the races as they considered necessary to keep a Negro man's legs

from coming too close to a white woman's knees" (*Parting the Waters,* 14). Such racial concerns pervaded southern communities.

18. Mitch Ariff, "GHS Hornets Smash South Vicksburg, 55–6," *Delta Democrat-Times,* November 7, 1971, 10; Mitch Ariff, "GHS Scores Comeback Win over Greenwood," *Delta Democrat-Times,* November 14, 1971, 14.

19. Mitch Ariff, "Hornets Nip Callaway in 1st Capital Bowl," *Delta Democrat-Times,* November 28, 1971, 9.

20. "Dempsey Named Coach of Year," *Delta Democrat-Times,* November 29, 1971, 10.

21. "Five Hornets on North All-Big 8," *Delta Democrat-Times,* December 3, 1971, 7. The University of Arkansas Razorbacks heavily recruited Elliott Williams, but he chose to play football at the University of Texas at El Paso. Because he was more academically inclined, Williams' stay in West Texas was brief (Gary Dempsey, interview by Edward J. Robinson, July 15, 2010).

22. Mitch Ariff, "GHS Hornets Upset by Tupelo, 19–14," *Delta Democrat-Times,* September 10, 1972, 14.

23. Mitch Ariff, "Hornets Attempt New Win Streak," *Delta Democrat-Times,* September 14, 1972, 11.

24. Mitch Ariff, "Hornets Hold on to Defeat Pine Bluff," *Delta Democrat-Times,* September 17, 1972, 12.

25. Wally Wilson, "Hornets Sting Wildcats," *Delta Democrat-Times,* October 1, 1972, 13.

26. Mitch Ariff, "Hornets Hold on to Defeat Meridian," *Delta Democrat-Times,* October 8, 1972, 15.

27. Mitch Ariff, "Hornets Defeat Highly Rated Airline," *Delta Democrat-Times,* October 15, 1972, 15.

28. Mitch Ariff, "Hornets Score Decisive Win over Lee," *Delta Democrat-Times,* October 29, 1972, 14.

29. Mitch Ariff, "Hornets Upset Clarksdale to S[t]ay in Race," *Delta Democrat-Times,* November 5, 1972, 14.

30. Mitch Ariff, "Hornets Win Grudge Battle over 'Dogs," *Delta Democrat-Times,* November 19, 1972, 17.

31. "Hornets Get Share of Title," *Delta Democrat-Times,* November 19, 1972, 20.

32. "Four Hornets on All-Big 8," *Delta Democrat-Times,* December 7, 1972, 15.

33. Dempsey, interview, July 6, 2010.

34. Dent, "What's a Country Boy Like Wilbert Doing at Super-Hype Bowl?" 4.

35. Dempsey, interview, July 24, 2009.

Chapter 3

1. Wilbert Montgomery, interview by Edward J. Robinson, December 8, 2008.

2. Ponto Downing, "Abilene Team Gives Jackson St. 'Lesson' in Football Recruiting," *Clarion-Ledger,* December 8, 1973, B-1.

3. Pearlman, *Sweetness,* 100.

4. Downing, "Abilene Team Gives Jackson St. 'Lesson,' " B-1.

5. Mark McDonald, "The Sinister Story of Wilbert's 'Abduction,' " *Abilene Reporter News,* December 20, 1973, 5-C.

6. Art Lawler, "Honing Their Skills on the Delta," *Abilene Reporter News,* August 31, 1975, 5-F.

7. Odis Dolton, interview by Edward J. Robinson, April 8, 2010.

8. Randy Scott, interview by Edward J. Robinson, April 5, 2010.

9. Bill Hart, "Focus," *Abilene Reporter News,* February 11, 1979, 5-C.

10. Quoted in Pearlman, *Sweetness,* 100.

11. Mark Wilson, "He Couldn't Say No," *Abilene Reporter News,* August 4, 1996, 5-D; Wilbert Montgomery, interview, December 8, 2008.

12. Lawler, "Honing Their Skills on the Delta," 5-F; and Wilson, "He Couldn't Say No," 5-D. Bob Hill is quoted in Pearlman, *Sweetness,* 100. It is noteworthy that Wilbert Montgomery's portrayal of the Jackson State coaching staff differed markedly from Walter Payton's view of coach Bob Hill. Payton acknowledged that he chose to enroll at Jackson State because of his brother Eddie and because of Bob Hill, whose practices were often grueling and who treated "you like a parent. He probably would have taken you out and spanked your butt just like a parent would do." See Payton and Yaeger, *Never Die Easy,* 55 (quotation), 57, 66.

13. Andrew Williams is quoted in McDonald, "The Sinister Story of Wilbert's Abduction," 1-C; Wilson, "He Couldn't Say No," 5-D.

14. Wally Bullington, interview by Edward J. Robinson, April 14, 2010; Art Lawler, "Catching a Star," *Abilene Reporter News,* December 12, 1973, 3-C.

15. Al Pickett, "Payton Played Role in Montgomery Coming to ACU," *Abilene Reporter News,* November 4, 1999, 1-C. Jeff Pearlman writes, "According to Hill, Jackson, [Mississippi] was home to a wealthy Abilene booster with a private jet who had been snooping around campus, whispering sweet nothings to Montgomery" (*Sweetness,* 100).

16. Lawler, "Catching a Star," 3-C.

17. Pickett, "Payton Played a Role in Montgomery Coming to ACU," 1-C.

18. Wilson, "He Couldn't Say No," 5-D.

19. Addie Felts, interview by Edward J. Robinson, March 25, 2010. See also Lopez, *Cougars of Any Color,* 80.

20. Wright, "The Ethics of Living Jim Crow."

21. Cobb, *The Most Southern Place on Earth,* 218–19. See also Hudson-Weems, *Emmett Till;* and Litwack, *Trouble in Mind.*

22. Felts, interview. Jerry LeVias, the first African American football player at SMU, had a similar experience in Dallas, where Burt and Elsie Flashnick, a Jewish couple, "adopted" him and treated him "as an equal at the pinnacle of society" (Pennington, *Breaking the Ice,* 100).

23. McDonald, "The Sinister Story of Wilbert's 'Abduction,' " 1-D.

24. Felts, interview.

25. Felts, interview.

26. John C. Whitley, interview by Edward J. Robinson, June 29, 2010. Not all coaches and staff members at "Christian" colleges and universities embraced black players enthusiastically. John Westbrook remembered some coaches at Baptist-affiliated Baylor University as "hateful and vindictive." Jerry LeVias recalled that one of Hayden Fry's assistant coaches at SMU complained, "Come on, you guys are moving around like a bunch of lazy niggers" (Pennington, *Breaking the Ice,* 75, 104). Additionally, scholar Katherine Lopez reminds us that the "spirit of Jim Crow" pervaded the stands at game time (*Cougars of Any Color,* 140). Not only was this true at a public university, the University of Houston, but it could also be true at a religious institution.

27. See Harrison and Lampman, "The Image of Paul Robeson," 117–20; Dave Merrell, interview by Edward J. Robinson, March 30, 2010.

28. Regrettably, I was unsuccessful in getting a copy of the picture for this book. However, the picture appears in *Abilene Reporter News,* December 6, 1973, 6-A. Randy Scott, interview by Edward J. Robinson, February 17, 2012.

29. Wilson, "He Couldn't Say No," 4-D. Just as Warren McVea enrolled at the University of Houston in 1964 because he "trusted" coach Bill Yeoman, Wilbert Montgomery trusted the coaching staff at ACC. For the observation about McVea, see Lopez, *Cougars of Any Color,* 73.

30. "Window Fastest Way to ACU for Wilbert," *Abilene Reporter News,* December 27, 1979, 1-C. Giles, after playing high football for the Greenville Hornets, starred at Alcorn State University before being drafted by the Houston Oilers in 1977. He then played for the Tampa Bay Buccaneers (1978–1986), the Detroit Lions (1986–1987), and the Philadelphia Eagles (1987–1989).

31. Garner Roberts, "Montgomery Inducted into College Football Hall of Fame," *Abilene Reporter News,* August 18, 1996, 4-D.

Chapter 4

1. Mark McDonald, "ACC Wildcats Begin New Era in LSC," *Abilene Reporter News,* September 2, 1973, 14-F.

2. McDonald, "ACC Wildcats Begin New Era in LSC," 14-F.

3. Wally Bullington, interview by Edward J. Robinson, April 14, 2010 (Bullington was ACC's head football coach and athletic director from 1969 to 1988. [Stevens, *No Ordinary University,* 37–38]); Hubert Pickett, interview by Edward J. Robinson, March 12, 2010; Ove Johansson, interview by Edward J. Robinson, April 15, 2010; Bob Strader, interview by Edward J. Robinson, July 21, 2010.

4. McDonald, "ACC Wildcats Begin New Era in LSC," 14-F.

5. "More Honors for ACC Duo," *Abilene Reporter News,* January 1, 1974.

6. Mark McDonald, " 'Rapid Richard' Is Back," *Abilene Reporter News,* September 4, 1973, 1-C.

7. Mark McDonald, "ASU Edges ACC in Wild One," *Abilene Reporter News*, September 9, 1973, 1-C.

8. "Five Wildcats Honored, Bullington Coach of Year," *Abilene Reporter News*, December 2, 1973, 3-C.

9. "Optimist Player of the Week," *Optimist*, October 26, 1973, 7.

10. "Five Wildcats Honored, Bullington Coach of Year," 3-C.

11. Mark McDonald, "ACC Seeks Answers," *Abilene Reporter News*, September 1, 1973, 1-C.

12. McDonald, "ACC Wildcats Begin New Era in LSC," 14-F.

13. Wilbert Montgomery is quoted in Judy Hammons, "Wally, Wilbert Say ACC a 'Team,'" *Abilene Reporter News*, December 6, 1973, 6-A. See also "ACC's Unknown Is Now Reknown [*sic*]," *Abilene Reporter News*, December 7, 1973, 1-C.

14. McDonald, "ASU Edges ACC in Wild One."

15. Mark McDonald, "ACC's Steady Cowboy," *Abilene Reporter News*, September 11, 1973, 1-C.

16. Mark McDonald, "Laminack Back 'Home,'" *Abilene Reporter News*, September 4, 1973, 1-C.

17. Mark McDonald, "Soft Sound, Hard Hits," *Abilene Reporter News*, September 25, 1973, 2-C.

18. Mark McDonald, "ACC Swarms Past A&I, 35–14," *Abilene Reporter News*, September 23, 1973, 1-C.

19. Mark McDonald, "Longley Passes ACC to 41–7 Victory," *Abilene Reporter News*, September 30, 1973, 1-C.

20. Mark McDonald, "ACC Fans Boost Wildcat Mania," *Abilene Reporter News*, December 4, 1973, 2-C.

21. Bullington, interview.

22. Curtis Culwell, "Cats Strong Title Contenders," *Optimist*, September 7, 1973, 12.

23. Mark McDonald, "Montgomery Shines," *Abilene Reporter News*, August 25, 1973.

24. Mark McDonald, "'Three-Ring Circus' Sees Strong Defense," *Abilene Reporter News*, September 2, 1973, 1-C.

25. "ACC Enrollment Reaches 3,190," *Abilene Reporter News*, September 6, 1973, 1-B.

26. John C. Whitley, interview by Edward J. Robinson, June 29, 2010. See also Charles Orbison, "John Whitley: Black Pioneer," *Optimist*, September 10, 1971, 3; "Jones Named Visiting Professor," *Optimist*, April 27, 1973, 4. Henry Willis, a native of Levelland, Texas, transferred from Howard County Junior College in Big Spring (Brandon Tripp, "Breaking the ACU Color Barrier: Integration of ACU Sports Promotes Stronger Teams, Peaceful Community," *Optimist*, May 1, 2009, 11; Colter Hettich, "First African-American Student Recalls Struggle," *Optimist*, May 1, 2009, 5).

27. Gallaway, "A History of the Desegregation of the Public Schools in Abilene, Texas," 68 (quotation from black parent), 97 (quotation from Shults). See also Barr, *Black Texans*, especially chapter 5, "Outsiders."

28. "Arthur Smith Conducts Seminar," *Optimist,* February 19, 1973, 8. See also "Seminar in Interracial Relations by Dr. Smith Concludes Today," *Optimist,* March 9, 1973, 1; and "Arthur L. Smith, Lecturer, Raps on Transracial Roles," *Optimist,* March 16, 1973, 5.

29. Brit Chism, "Letter to the Editor," *Optimist,* March 9, 1973, 2.

30. Addie Felts, interview by Edward J. Robinson, March 25, 2010.

31. Pickett, interview.

32. Bullington, interview.

33. McDonald, "ASU Edges ACC in Wild One," 1.

34. McDonald, "ACC Swarms Past A&I, 35–14," 1.

35. Bill Hart, "Defense Wins Bet, ACC Shells A&I with Offense," *Abilene Reporter News,* September 23, 1973, 1.

36. Hart, "Defense Wins Bet," 1.

37. Hart, "Defense Wins Bet," 1.

38. McDonald, "Longley Passes ACC to 41–7 Victory," 1-C.

39. Curtis Culwell, "ACC Routs SWT 41–7," *Optimist,* October 5, 1973, 8.

40. Curtis Culwell, "ACC Scores Third Conference Victory," *Optimist,* October 12, 1973, 6; and "Optimist Player of the Week," *Optimist,* October 12, 1973, 8.

41. "Faces in the Crowd," *Sports Illustrated,* November 12, 1973, 115.

42. "ACC's Unknown Is Now Reknown [*sic*]," 1-C; Curtis Culwell, "Homecoming Victory 29–0," *Optimist,* October 26, 1973, 8.

43. Curtis Culwell, "Cats Shut Out Angelo 27–0," *Optimist,* November 2, 1973, 6.

44. Curtis Culwell, "Cats Club Texans 49–7," *Optimist,* November 9, 1973, 8.

45. Curtis Culwell, "ACC Slices SHSU 46–23," *Optimist,* November 16, 1973, 8.

46. Curtis Culwell, "Cats Dump Payne, 42–14," *Optimist,* November 30, 1973, 6.

47. "ACC's Unknown Is Now Reknown [*sic*]," 1-C.

48. McDonald, "ACC Wildcats Begin New Era in LSC," 14-F.

49. Denne H. Freeman, "Wilbert Montgomery Featured in AP Story," *Abilene Reporter News,* December 1, 1973, 1.

50. Freeman, "Wilbert Montgomery Featured in AP Story," 1.

51. Tom Mauldin and Bill Hart, "The Players' View," *Abilene Reporter News,* December 2, 1973, 1-C.

52. Mauldin and Hart, "The Players' View," 1-C.

53. Art Lawler, "Langston Fans' Emotions Boil," *Abilene Reporter News,* December 2, 1973, 1-C.

54. Bill Roberts, "Shreveport Here They Come," *Abilene Reporter News,* December 2, 1973, 1-C.

55. Lawler, "Langston Fans' Emotions Boil," 1-C.

56. Mauldin and Hart, "The Players' View," 1-C. For Thomas Henderson's reflection on the 1973 contest between the ACC Wildcats and the Langston Lions, see Henderson and Knobler, *Out of Control,* 55–56.

57. Lawler, "Langston Fans' Emotions Boil," 1-C.

58. "ACC Prepares for Title," *Abilene Reporter News,* December 1973, 2-C.

59. Mark McDonald, "Title Tilt a Waltz for Wildcats," *Abilene Reporter News,* December 9, 1973, 1-C, 3-C; "Abilene Christian Guns Down Elon for Title, 42–14," *The NAIA News,* Winter 1974, 4. Montgomery's asthma attack during the championship game seemed to have been a temporary problem, for it never surfaced again as a chronic problem. His leg injuries, however, would prove to be more lingering and more debilitating.

60. "Five Wildcats Honored, Bullington Coach of Year," *Abilene Reporter News,* December 2, 1973.

61. Barr, *Black Texans,* chapter 5.

62. Dave Merrell, interview by Edward J. Robinson, March 30, 2010.

63. Whitley, interview. Charles Hodge, letter Edward J. Robinson, July 17, 2010. In the author's possession.

64. Rena Wright, interview by Edward J. Robinson, April 14, 2010.

65. Bissinger, *Friday Night Lights,* 108.

Chapter 5

1. Art Lawler, "Repeat '73—Forget It," *Abilene Reporter News,* December 6, 1974, 1-E.

2. Mark McDonald, "Wildcats Deer Hunting," *Abilene Reporter News,* November 30, 1974, 6-D.

3. Wilbert Montgomery, interview by Edward J. Robinson, June 16, 2010. When recently asked about this incident, neither then-coach Wally Bullington nor former football player Bob Strader remembered this conflict between Wilbert Montgomery and Gary Graham. Yet Montgomery and the *Abilene Reporter News* confirm that it happened.

4. Edwards, *The Revolt of the Black Athlete,* 26. Hall of Fame running back Jim Brown has pointed out that the National Football League wanted "nice guy blacks, humble blacks . . . who wouldn't rock the status quo" (Brown and Delsohn, *Out of Bounds,* 56). For Jim Brown's criticism of coach Paul Brown and Cleveland Browns, see also Ross, *Outside the Lines,* 139. For discussion of NFL coaches' alarm over black "troublemakers," see Brower, "The Black Side of Football," 130–66.

   For the Joe Louis reference, see O. Edmonds, "Joe Louis, Boxing, and American Culture," 137–38. For an insightful comparison between Jack Johnson and Joe Louis, see Roberts, *Joe Louis,* 41–51 (The insightful quotation is on 51). For thorough treatments of Jack Johnson's meteoric and controversial career, see Roberts, *Papa Jack;* and Geoffrey C. Ward, *Unforgivable Blackness.* For the observation concerning whites' expectations of Don Chaney, Elvin Hayes, and Warren McVea, see Lopez, *Cougars of Any Color,* 135.

5. Wilbert Montgomery, interview, June 16, 2010.

6. Mark McDonald, "Odds against ACC Repeat," *Abilene Reporter News,* September 1, 1974, 14-F. Dave Merrell, interview by Edward J. Robinson, March 30, 2010. Bob Strader, interview by Edward J. Robinson, July 21, 2010. The term "scholar-baller"

is borrowed from: Harrison and Lampman, "The Image of Paul Robeson," 117–30. Paul Robeson was a scholar-baller who used athletics to achieve academic goals.

7. Bill Hart, "Cleotha's An All-Star," *Abilene Reporter News,* May 10, 1974, 1-C; Bill Hart, "3 M's Together Again," *Abilene Reporter News,* August 7, 1974, 1-C.

8. "11 Wildcats Post 4.7 or Faster Timings," *Abilene Reporter News,* August 20, 1974, 1-C; McDonald, "Odds against ACC Repeat," 14-F.

9. Rick Hagar, "Snake Hunter Gives Insight in Longley's Switch to Dallas," *Optimist,* September 6, 1974, 8; McDonald, "Odds against ACC Repeat," 14-F. ACC officials "booted" Hubert Pickett from school for fighting. See "Wildcat Back Loses Suspension Appeal," *Abilene Reporter News,* June 29, 1974, 1-C; Bill Hart, "Pickett Is ACC's 'Comeback of Year' Man," *Abilene Reporter News,* November 5, 1975, 1-E.

10. Ray Donley, "Clee's Football Debut Impressive," *Optimist,* September 13, 1974, 8; Mark Flippin, "Wildcats Overcome Problems to Top SCA Bears," *Optimist,* September 13, 1974, 8.

11. Art Lawler, "'Cats Erase Doubts—Finally," *Abilene Reporter News,* September 22, 1974, 1-C; "Wilbert Named Player of the Week," *Abilene Reporter News,* September 25, 1974,

12. "Upset Virus Inflicts Wildcats," *Optimist,* October 4, 1974, 8.

13. Paula Holland, "Stocker, Stirman Selected Top Wildcats of Week," *Optimist,* October 11, 1974, 8.

14. Dan Marton, "Cats Look to East Texas for Revenge," *Optimist,* October 18, 1974, 12.

15. Mark McDonald, "Wildcats Trample East Texas, 31–13," *Abilene Reporter News,* October 20, 1974, 1-C; "Cats Stomp Lions," *Optimist,* October 25, 1974, 8.

16. Dan Martin, "Easy Game Slated at Alpine," *Optimist,* October 25, 1974, 7; Mark McDonald, "ACC Drops Sul Ross," *Abilene Reporter News,* October 27, 1974, 1-C.

17. Mark McDonald, "Wildcats Claw Angelo State, 33–21," *Abilene Reporter News,* November 3, 1974, 1-C; Art Lawler, "Fans Get Dollars' Worth," *Abilene Reporter News,* November 3, 1974.

18. Mark McDonald, "ACC Routs Tarleton," *Abilene Reporter News,* November 10, 1974, 2-C.

19. Mark McDonald, "ACC Clips Sam Houston, 33–24," *Abilene Reporter News,* November 17, 1974, 2-C.

20. Mark McDonald, "Howard Payne Spills ACC, 42–21," *Abilene Reporter News.* November 24, 1974, 1-C.

21. Bill Hart, "Howard Payne QB 'Rubbed It In,'" *Abilene Reporter News,* November 25, 1974, 1-C.

22. McDonald, "Wildcats Deer Hunting," 6-D.

23. Scott Kirk, "Wildcats, Bears Forfeit Due to Eligibility Status," *Optimist,* October 25, 1974, 8.

24. McDonald, "Wildcats Deer Hunting," 6-D.

Chapter 6

1. Art Lawler, "Fellow Fool," *Abilene Reporter News,* February 13, 1975, 1-C.
2. Bill Hart, "Good Old No. 28," *Abilene Reporter News,* March 14, 1975, 2-C.
3. Bill Hart, "Spinsters [*sic*] Emerging," *Abilene Reporter News,* April 1, 1975.
4. "100 ACC Candidates Report for Workouts," *Abilene Reporter News,* August 21, 1975, 11-C.
5. "Wildcats Start Workouts, Another Starter Pulls Out," *Abilene Reporter News,* August 23, 1975, 5-C.
6. "Wildcats Happy about Tough Opener," *Abilene Reporter News,* September 7, 1975, 4-C.
7. Art Lawler, "ACC Opens against Troy State," *Abilene Reporter News,* September 13, 1975, 3-C.
8. Art Lawler, "Abilene Christian Hammers Troy State, 34–7," *Abilene Reporter News,* September 14, 1975, 1-C.
9. Art Lawler, "ACC Concluding Remarks," *Abilene Reporter News,* September 16, 1975, 1-C.
10. Lawler, "ACC Concluding Remarks," 1-C.
11. "Wildcats 'Restrict' Star Running Back," *Abilene Reporter News,* September 21, 1975, 4-C.
12. Ray Donley and Rick Hagar, "Montgomery Suspended, Reinstated," *Optimist,* September 26, 1975, 1.
13. Bill Hart, "ACC Has Own Water(gun) Gate," *Abilene Reporter News,* September 23, 1975. See also Jan Moulden, "ACC Silent on Montgomery Case," *Abilene Reporter News,* October 1, 1975, 2-C.
14. Edwards has pointed out that thirty seven black athletic revolts occurred on predominantly white university campuses in 1968 alone (*Revolt of the Black Athlete,* 88).
15. Moulden, "ACC Silent on Montgomery Case," 2-C.
16. Wilbert Montgomery, interview by Edward J. Robinson, June 16, 2010.
17. Dave Merrell, interview by Edward J. Robinson, March 30, 2010; Odis Dolton, interview by Edward J. Robinson, April 8, 2010.
18. Bill Hart, "Texas A&I Uses Late Break to Down ACC," *Abilene Reporter News,* September 28, 1975, 1-C; Michael Hurley, "Wildcats Drop Heartbreaker to A&I," *Optimist,* October 3, 1975, 5.
19. Art Lawler, " 'Cats Face Southwest Texas," *Abilene Reporter News,* October 4, 1975, 2-C.
20. Art Lawler, "Southwest Texas Stops Abilene Christian, 21–16," *Abilene Reporter News,* October 5, 1975, 2-C.
21. Bill Hart, "ACC Rips S. F. Austin, 24–3," *Abilene Reporter News,* October 12, 1975, 2-C.
22. Art Lawler, "Wounded Wildcats Try East Texas," *Abilene Reporter News,* October 18, 1975, 6-C.

23. Art Lawler, "East Texas Holds Off Wildcat Rally, 20–18," *Abilene Reporter News,* October 19, 1975, 1-C.

24. Bill Hart, " 'Cat Stars to Miss Sul Ross," *Abilene Reporter News,* October 25, 1975, 6-C.

25. Bill Roberts, "Wildcats Dance . . . Score . . . and Score," *Abilene Reporter News,* October 25, 1975, 1-C.

26. Art Lawler, "Wildcats' Brew Lacks Victory," *Abilene Reporter News,* November 2, 1975, 1-C.

27. Bill Hart, "Abilene Christian Blunts Tarleton Threat," *Abilene Reporter News,* November 9, 1975, 1-C.

28. Bill Hart, "ACC Rolls Past Sam Houston State, 55–20," *Abilene Reporter News,* November 16, 1975, 1-C.

29. "Wilbert Honored by LSC," *Abilene Reporter News,* November 17, 1975, 1-C.

30. Art Lawler, "Blood Boils for ACC-HPU," *Abilene Reporter News,* November 22, 1975, 2-C.

31. Lawler, "Blood Boils for ACC-HPU," 2-C.

32. Art Lawler, "ACC Explodes Past Howard Payne," *Abilene Reporter News,* November 23, 1975, 1-C.

33. Bill Hart, "Wildcats Warm, Loose, Playing for Memories," *Abilene Reporter News,* November 23, 1975, 5-C.

34. Mark Flippin, "Perkins Ends Banner Season," *Optimist,* December 5, 1975, 10.

35. Art Lawler, "Perkins? He's the Bestest," *Abilene Reporter News,* November 26, 1975, 1-C.

Chapter 7

1. Hargrove, *Jimmy Carter as President.*

2. Darla Parker, "Change to University Causes Hassles," *Optimist,* March 5, 1976, 5; "Enrollment Now over 3,800," *Optimist,* September 10, 1976, 6; "ACU Enrollment Establishes Record," *Abilene Reporter News,* September 16, 1976, 10-A.

3. Art Lawler, "Wildcats Win in Romp, 48–14," *Abilene Reporter News,* September 5, 1976, 1-C; Bill Roberts, "Labhart Leads Ho-Hum Romp over NWOSU," *Optimist,* September 10, 1976, 10.

4. Art Lawler, " 'Cats Persevere in Dying Seconds to Win," *Abilene Reporter News,* September 12, 1976, 1-C.

5. Ron Hadfield, "UNC Halted by Impressive Wildcat Defense," *Optimist,* September 17, 1976, 10.

6. Art Lawler, " 'Cats Hold on for Half, Then Succumb," *Abilene Reporter News,* September 26, 1976, 1-C.

7. Ron Hadfield, "Behavior of A&I Fans Blasted," *Optimist,* October 1, 1976, 11.

8. Art Lawler, "Would You Believe 21–16—Again?" *Abilene Reporter News,* October 3, 1976, 1-C.

9. "ACU Injury List Is Enough to Make You Cry," *Abilene Reporter News,* October 9, 1976, 3-C.

10. "Wildcats Come Back," *Abilene Reporter News,* October 10, 1976, 5-C.

11. Ron Hadfield, "Improving Wildcats Ready for ETSU," *Optimist,* October 16, 1976, 12.

12. Ove Johansson, interview by Edward J. Robinson, April 15, 2010.

13. Art Lawler, "Johansson's 69-Yarder Helps ACU Win, 17–0," *Abilene Reporter News,* October 17, 1976, 1-C; Ron Hadfield, "Wilbert, Ove Set Records as Wildcats Defeat ET," *Optimist,* October 22, 1976, 12. Johansson's sixty-nine yard field goal has yet to be surpassed.

14. Ron Hadfield, "Ove Confused over Importance of His Field Goal," *Optimist,* October 22, 1976, 11.

15. Art Lawler, "Reese Has Fantastic Home Finale in Win," *Abilene Reporter News,* October 31, 1976, 1-C. See also Ron Hadfield, "Reese: 'This Is Ridiculous'; Angelo Attitudes Criticized," *Optimist,* November 5, 1976, 11. The LSC bestowed "Player of the Week" honors on Reese for his astounding performance ("Reese Honored," *Abilene Reporter News,* November 1, 1976, 1-C).

16. Scott Kirk, "These Two Roomies Partners in Violence," *Optimist,* October 16, 1976, 10.

17. Bob Lapham, "ACU Has It Easy," *Abilene Reporter News,* November 7, 1976, 2-C; "ACU Defense Keeps Shining," *Abilene Reporter News,* November 14, 1976, 3-C.

18. Ron Hadfield, "Davis Learns from Montgomery," *Optimist,* November 19, 1976, 11.

19. Art Lawler, "Wildcats Gain Berth in San Jacinto Bowl," *Abilene Reporter News,* November 21, 1976, 1-C.

20. Ron Hadfield, "Tribute to Montgomery Inspires Football Team," *Optimist,* December 10, 1976, 11.

21. Art Lawler, "Wildcats Triumph in Shrine Bowl," *Abilene Reporter News,* December 5, 1976, 1-C; Ron Hadfield, "Wildcats Too Much for Harding in Shrine Bowl," *Optimist,* December 10, 1976, 12.

22. Hadfield, "Tribute to Montgomery Inspires Football Team," 11.

23. Randy Scott, interview by Edward J. Robinson, April 5, 2010.

24. On the racism African American athletes Warren McVea, John Westbrook, and Jerry LeVias encountered at the University of Houston, Baylor University, and Southern Methodist University, see Pennington, *Breaking the Ice,* 32, 75, 92, 95.

25. G. P. Holt, "Tension between the Black and White Church," *Christian Echo,* June 1969, 4, 9. See also Hughes, *Reviving the Ancient Faith,* 292.

26. Scott, interview, April 5, 2010. In the mid-1960s in Houston, Texas, basketball player Don Chaney was denied entrance into movie theaters and other public establishments. "You guys can [come in]," one restaurant thundered, "but not the Nigger" (Lopez, *Cougars of Any Color,* 85).

27. Bob Strader, interview by Edward J. Robinson, July 21, 2010.

28. On February 21, 1974, Wilbert Montgomery was named honorary chairman of the Abilene Association for Retarded Children. See *Abilene Reporter News,* February 22, 1974, 8-A. Regrettably, I was not able to get a copy of the photo.

Chapter 8

1. The New England Patriots were especially interested in picking Wilbert Montgomery because they believed him to be a good compliment to their power runner, Sam Cunningham. Yet the Patriots spurned him after learning that he had "suffered a severe thigh injury at one time and a calcium deposit remained. It was, New England scouts decided, too high a risk." Because of his leg injury, Montgomery's forty-yard dash time dropped from 4.4 to 4.5 seconds, convincing Patriot coach, Chuck Fairbanks, that the former ACC star was not fully ready for the NFL. See Carlton Stowers, "Montgomery Adds Octane to Eagles," *Dallas Morning News,* November 8, 1979, 1-B; Forbes, *Dick Vermeil,* 73. During his rookie season, Montgomery explained the reason behind his frequent injuries, stating, "I missed five games my senior year, three games my junior year, three more the year before. What the scouts didn't see was that the guys on the line in front of me were really light and I was running the ball a lot. I really took a beating" (Dick Weiss, "Wilbert A 4-TD Smash," *Philadelphia Daily News,* September 11, 1978, 79).

   For the cultural and historical significance of Philadelphia, Pennsylvania, see Lane, *William Dorsey's Philadelphia and Ours,* 340–342, 346–348; Blockson, *Philadelphia,* 147.
2. Payton and Yaeger, *Never Die Easy.*
3. Singletary and Jenkins, *Singletary on Singletary.*
4. Blount and Sterling, *The Cross Burns Brightly.*
5. Barkley and Wilbon, *I May Be Wrong.*
6. Smith, "Bill Russell: Pioneer and Champion of the Sixties," 234; Blount and Sterling, *The Cross Burns Brightly,* 24, 27. For an excellent overview of the African Americans' struggle to desegregate the NFL, see Ross, *Outside the Lines.*
7. Barkley and Wilbon, *I May Be Wrong,* 47–48. For further insight into the history of racial discrimination in the City of Brotherly Love, see the story of Cecil B. Moore, a president of Philadelphia's NAACP, who led the fight against social inequality and racial injustice in Willis, *Cecil's City.*
8. Dorsett and Frommer, *Running Tough,* 49; Phillips, *White Metropolis,* 167.
9. Jim Dent, "Montgomery Developed Elusiveness Off Field Too," *Dallas Times Herald,* January 23, 1981, 7. In another source, Montgomery said that "seven guys" harassed him and his friends by throwing beer cans and by damaging their vehicle. "There were seven guys in the other car. They began throwing beer cans at us. We came to a stoplight and one of the guys jumped on the back of our car and started beating on the trunk" (Forbes, *Dick Vermeil,* 74).
10. Ralph Bernstein, "Wilbert: 'I Never Thought I'd Make It,'" *Abilene Reporter News,*

September 16, 1984, 3-C. For quotations from Montgomery Vermeil quotes, see Forbes, *Dick Vermeil,* 72–73.

11. Ron Hadfield, "Wilbert's Example Could Change a Life," *Optimist,* September 9, 1997, 2.

12. Bruce Lowitt, "Wilbert Gaining Attention," *Abilene Reporter News,* October 19, 1978, 1-C.

13. "Montgomery Runs over Miami Defense," *Abilene Reporter News,* September 25, 1978, 3-C.

14. "Wilbert Scores Winning TD Win over Colts," *Abilene Reporter News,* October 2, 1978, 3-B.

15. Art Lawler, "A 'Hick from the Sticks' Discovered," *Abilene Reporter News,* October 19, 1978, 1-C.

16. Significantly, Johnny Perkins, Wilbert Montgomery's former teammate at ACU, caught three passes for sixty-five yards and a touchdown during the so-called Miracle at the Meadowlands.

17. Dave Brady, "Eagles Beat Giants to Reach Playoffs," *Washington Post,* December 18, 1978, D-1. Steve Van Buren, a first-round pick out of LSU by the Eagles in 1944, led Philadelphia to three playoff appearances and two NFL championships (in 1948 and 1949) in his eight-year career. Van Buren died recently at the age of ninety-one. See "For the Record," *Sports Illustrated,* September 3, 2012, 16.

18. "Eagles Clinch Berth," *Abilene Reporter News,* December 18, 1978, 1-C.

19. "Staubach, Campbell Named All-Pro," *Abilene Reporter News,* December 15, 1978, 2-C; Bill Hart, "Focus," *Abilene Reporter News,* February 11, 1979, 5-C.

20. "Wilbert's Bank Account Balloons," *Abilene Reporter News,* July 17, 1979, 2-C; "Montgomery Signs 5-Year Pact Said Worth $1.5 Million," *Abilene Reporter News,* July 18, 1979, 4-C.

21. "Wilbert Runs over 'Skins," *Abilene Reporter News,* October 8, 1978, 2-C.

22. "Eagles' Vermeil All Smiles," *Abilene Reporter News,* October 9, 1979, 3-C.

23. "Eagles Continue Winning," *Abilene Reporter News,* October 15, 1979, 2-D.

24. "Browns Rally Past Eagles," *Abilene Reporter News,* November 5, 1979, 1-B. Additionally, in the loss against the Cleveland Browns, Harold Carmichael, a 6'8" receiver for the Philadelphia Eagles, broke an NFL record by catching a pass in his 106th consecutive game. A native of Jacksonville, Florida, and a product of the predominantly black Southern University in Louisiana, Carmichael played thirteen seasons with the Philadelphia Eagles (1971–1983) and one with the Dallas Cowboys. See "Carmichael Sets Receiving Record," *Abilene Reporter News,* November 5, 1979, 3-B; "Carmichael Sets Record in Eagles' 24–19 Loss, *Abilene Reporter News,* November 6, 1979, 1-C.

25. "Friends, Family Praise Montgomery," *Abilene Reporter News,* November 12, 1979, 3-C.

26. "Friends, Family Praise Montgomery," 3-C.

27. Bill Hart, "Eagles Dump Cowboys' Comeback Try," *Abilene Reporter News,* November 13, 1979, 1-C.

28. Neil Warner, "Best Late-Round Draftees of '70s," *Pro Football Weekly,* August 25, 1980, 18. Other late-round draftees on the *PFW* "Dream Team" included Jean Fugett, Stan Walters, David Taylor, Herbert Scott, Conrad Dobler, Mike Webster, Harold Carmichael, Mel Gray, Brian Sipe, and Roland Harper. The foregoing players were placed on the *PFW* "Dream Team" Offense. The defensive team consisted of Bob Pollard, Carl Hairston, Larry Brooks, Doug Sutherland, Ray Hamilton, Dick Ambrose, Stan White, John Bunting, Lemar Parrish, Joe Lavender, Jake Scott, and Mike Wagner. Specialists were Bob Grupp, Mark Moseley, and Billy "White Shoes" Johnson.

29. Joel Buchsbaum, "NFL Player Ratings," *Pro Football Weekly,* August 25, 1980, 38.

30. "Wilbert Leads Eagles, 35–3," *Abilene Reporter News,* September 23, 1980, 1-C.

31. Art Lawler, "Cowboys Win Battle, Eagles Take War," *Abilene Reporter News,* December 22, 1980, 1-C.

32. "Eagles Turn over Vikings, 31–16," *Abilene Reporter News,* January 4, 1981, 1-C; "Wilbert Comes Back," *Abilene Reporter News,* January 4, 1981, 4-C.

33. "Cowboys, Eagles Nearly Identical," *Abilene Reporter News,* January 11, 1981, 1-C.

34. "Montgomery, Eagles Run over Dallas," *Abilene Reporter News,* January 12, 1981, 1-B; "Wilbert Keys Eagle Victory," *Abilene Reporter News,* January 12, 1981, 3-C; Red Smith, "Philadelphia Story," *New York Times* January 12, 1981, C-1.

35. Hal Bock, "Eagles Confident," *Abilene Reporter News,* January 23, 1981, 2-C.

36. "Super Bowl Today," *Abilene Reporter News,* January 25, 1981, 1-C.

37. McDonnell, *The Football Game I'll Never Forget,* 154–155. Jim Plunkett was named MVP of the Super Bowl XV.

38. "Raiders End Story with Super Bowl Win," *Abilene Reporter News,* January 25, 1981, 1-B, 3-B.

39. "Vermeil Says Eagles Better Than Ever," *Abilene Reporter News,* September 3, 1981, 4-D.

40. "Wilbert Blasts Giants' Tactics," *Abilene Reporter News,* December 23, 1981.

41. "Wilbert Blasts Giants' Tactics."

42. Bill Hart, "Wilbert Dinner Plans Finalized," *Abilene Reporter News,* March 22, 1981, 4-C; Art Lawler, "ACU Heaps Honors on Ol' No. 28," *Abilene Reporter News,* March 28, 1981, 1-C, 4-C. Even though Wilbert Montgomery had serious doubts as to whether he would make the Philadelphia Eagles football team, he became more and more confident as he emerged as both the starting and featured running back for the Eagles. In many ways he shared the confidence of Gale Sayers, who expressed that he "wasn't cocky when [he] came to the Bears, but [he] knew [he] could play" (Whittingham, *What Bears They Were,* 15).

43. Mitch Albom, "Wilbert the Lion-Hearted May Be What Lions Need," *Detroit Free Press,* August 26, 1985.

44. "Montgomery Hangs 'Em Up," *Abilene Reporter News,* May 6, 1986, 1-C.

45. Bill Lyon, "A Fighter Whose Scars Will Be His Only Tribute," *The Philadelphia Inquirer,* August 22, 1985, 1-E.

46. Dave Brady, "Montgomery Thrives," *Washington Post,* October 18, 1979, D-1.

Chapter 9

1. Wilbert Montgomery, interview by Edward J. Robinson, October 26, 2010.
2. "Wilbert Montgomery in the Hall of Fame," *Wildcat Football,* 2008, 134. "ACU's Montgomery Is First Athlete Named to LSC Hall of Honor," *Abilene Reporter News,* October 11, 1996, 7-B.
3. R. B. Fallstrom, "Montgomery Lands Job on Vermeil's St. Louis Staff," *Abilene Reporter News,* January 25, 1997, 5-B.
4. Fallstrom, "Montgomery Lands Job on Vermeil's St. Louis Staff," 5-B.
5. Dave Kindred, "Fourteen Years Later, He's Refreshed," *The Sporting News,* April 28, 1997, 7.
6. Kindred, "Fourteen Years Later, He's Refreshed."
7. Derron Montgomery, interview by Edward J. Robinson, March 10, 2010. Derron Montgomery, Wilbert Montgomery's son, played football two years at Iowa State University before transferring to Abilene Christian University. Wilbert Montgomery, interview by Edward J. Robinson, June 16, 2010.
8. Wilbert Montgomery, interview, June 16, 2010.
9. Le'Ron McClain, interview by Edward J. Robinson, November 18, 2010; Willis McGahee, interview by Edward J. Robinson, November 19, 2010; Ray Rice, interview by Edward J. Robinson, December 17, 2010. Many thanks to Patrick M. Gleason, public relations manager for the Baltimore Ravens, for arranging these interviews for me. McClain currently plays with the Kansas City Chiefs, and McGahee is with the Denver Broncos.
10. Wilbert Montgomery shared these comments with *Clarion-Ledger* sports editor Rod Walker on the *Clarion-Ledger* website, accessed November 27, 2010, www.clarionledger.com. I thank my good friend Brian McKnight for pointing me to this interview.
11. Wilbert Montgomery, interview, June 16, 2010.

Epilogue

1. Bob Strader, interview by Edward J. Robinson, July 21, 2010.
2. Harrison and Lampman, "The Image of Paul Robeson," 117–30.
3. Jim Gehman, *"Then Gibbs Said to Riggins . . ."* 188–90.
4. Compare Wilbert Montgomery's NFL statistics in appendix 5 of this book with Floyd Little's stats at *Pro Football Hall of Fame,* accessed February 20, 2012, www.profootballhof.com.
5. Upon entering the NFL in 1977, Montgomery confessed to being baffled and confused by the terminology used in Philadelphia Eagles team meetings during his rookie season. See Forbes, *Dick Vermeil,* 72.
6. Forbes, *Dick Vermeil,* 64.

Bibliography

Special Collections

The Wilbert Montgomery File (Abilene Christian University, Abilene, TX).

Newspapers

Abilene Reporter News
Clarion-Ledger (Jackson, MS)
Christian Echo (Los Angeles)
Dallas Morning News
Dallas Times Herald
Delta Democrat-Times (Greenville, MS)
Detroit Free Press
New York Times
Philadelphia Daily News
Philadelphia Inquirer
The NAIA News (Kansas City, MO)
The Optimist (Abilene, TX)
Washington Post

Magazines

Pro Football Weekly
The Sporting News
Sports Illustrated

SportsWeek
Texas Football Newsmagazine
Wildcat Football

Books and Articles

Ashe, Arthur R., Jr. *A Hard Road to Glory: A History of the African-American Athlete Since 1946.* New York: Warner Books, 1988.

Ashe, Arthur, and Arnold Rampersad. *Days of Grace: A Memoir.* New York: Alfred Knopf, 1993.

Barkley, Charles, and Michael Wilbon. *I May Be Wrong, But I Doubt It.* New York: Random House, 2002.

Barr, Alwyn. *Black Texans: A History of African Americans in Texas, 1528–1995.* Norman: University of Oklahoma Press, 1996.

Barra, Allen. *The Last Coach: A Life of Paul "Bear" Bryant.* New York: W. W. Norton, 2005.

Bissinger, H. G. *Friday Night Lights: A Town, a Team, and a Dream.* Cambridge, MA: Da Capo Press, 2000.

Blair, Sam. *Earl Campbell: The Driving Force.* Waco, TX: Word Books, 1980.

Blockson, Charles L. *Philadelphia, 1639–2000.* Charleston, SC: Arcadia, 2000.

Blount, Mel, and Cynthia Sterling. *The Cross Burns Brightly: A Hall-of-Famer Tackles Racism and Adversity to Help Troubled Boys.* Grand Rapids, MI: Zondervan, 1993.

Branch, Taylor. *Parting the Waters: American in the King Years, 1954–1963.* New York: Simon & Schuster, 1988.

Brown, Jim, and Steve Delsohn. *Out of Bounds.* New York: Zebra Books, 1989.

Bullard, Sara. *Free at Last: A History of the Civil Rights Movement and Those Who Died in the Struggle.* New York: Oxford University Press, 1993.

Carroll, John M. *Red Grange and the Rise of Modern Football.* Urbana: University of Illinois Press, 1999.

Cobb, James C. *The Most Southern Place on Earth: The Mississippi Delta and the Roots of Regional Identity.* New York: Oxford University Press, 1992.

Cohn, David. *Where I Was Born and Raised.* South Bend, IN: University of Notre Dame Press, 1935.

Cunningham, Randall, and Steve Wartenberg. *I'm Still Scrambling.* New York: Doubleday, 1993.

Dollard, John. *Caste and Class in a Southern Town.* 3rd ed. New York: Doubleday Anchor Books, 1949.

Dorsett, Tony, and Harvey Frommer. *Running Tough: Memoirs of a Football Maverick.* New York: Doubleday, 1989.

Dyreson, Mark. "American Ideas about Race and Olympic Races from the 1890s to the 1950s: Shattering Myths or Reinforcing Scientific Racism?" *Journal of Sport History* 28 (Summer 2001): 173–215.

Edmonds, Anthony O. "Joe Louis, Boxing, and American Culture." In *Out of the Shadows: A Biographical History of African American Athletes,* edited by David K. Wiggins, 133–45. Fayetteville: University of Arkansas Press, 2006.

Edwards, Harry. *The Revolt of the Black Athlete.* New York: Free Press, 1970.

Eig, Jonathan. *Opening Day: The Story of Jackie Robinson's First Season.* New York: Simon & Schuster, 2007.

Fitzpatrick, Frank. *And the Walls Came Tumbling Down: Kentucky, Texas Western, and the Game That Changed American Sports.* New York: Simon & Schuster, 1999.

Forbes, Gordon. *Dick Vermeil: Whistle in His Mouth, Heart on His Sleeve.* Chicago: Triumph Books, 2009.

Freeman, Mike. *Jim Brown: The Fierce Life of an American Hero.* New York: Harper-Collins, 2006.

Gehman, Jim. *"Then Gibbs Said to Riggins . . .": The Best Washington Redskins Stories Ever Told.* Chicago: Triumph Books, 2009.

Graham, Tom, and Rachel Graham Cody. *Getting Open: The Unknown Story of Bill Garrett and the Integration of College Basketball.* New York: Atria Books, 2006.

Hargrove, Erwin C. *Jimmy Carter as President: Leadership and the Politics of the Public Good.* Baton Rouge: Louisiana State University Press, 1988.

Harrison, C. Keith, and Brian Lampman. "The Image of Paul Robeson: Role Model for the Student and Athlete." *Rethinking History* 5, no. 1 (2001): 117–30.

Henderson, Thomas "Hollywood," and Peter Knobler. *Out of Control: Confessions of an NFL Casualty.* New York: G. P. Putnam's Sons, 1987.

Hirsch, James S. *Willie Mays: The Life, The Legend.* New York: Scribner, 2010.

Hoberman, John. *Darwin's Athletes: How Sport Has Damaged Black America and Preserved the Myth of Race.* Boston: Houghton Mifflin, 1997.

Hudson-Weems, Clenora. *Emmett Till: The Sacrificial Lamb of the Civil Rights Movement.* Bloomington, IN: AuthorHouse, 2006.

Hughes, Richard T. *Reviving the Ancient Faith: The Story of Churches of Christ in America.* Grand Rapids, MI: Eerdmans, 1996.

Jaworski, Ron, Greg Cosell, and David Plaut. *The Games That Changed the Game: The Evolution of the NFL in Seven Sundays.* New York: Ballantine, 2011.

Johnson, Charles S. *Growing Up in the Black Belt: Negro Youth in the Rural South.* 1941. Reprint, New York: Schocken Books, 1967.

Lahman, Sean. *The Pro Football Historical Abstract: A Hardcore Fan's Guide to All-Time Player Rankings.* Guilford, CT: Lyons Press, 2008.

Lane, Roger. *William Dorsey's Philadelphia and Ours: On the Past and Future of the Black City in America.* New York: Oxford University Press, 1991.

Lee, Chana Kai. *For Freedom's Sake: The Life of Fannie Lou Hamer.* Urbana: University of Illinois Press, 1999.

Litwack, Leon F. *Trouble in Mind: Black Southerners in the Age of Jim Crow.* New York: Vintage, 1998.

Long, Michael G., ed. *First Class Citizenship: The Civil Rights Letters of Jackie Robinson.* New York: Henry Holt, 2007.

Lopez, Katherine. *Cougars of Any Color: The Integration of University of Houston Athletics, 1964–1968.* Jefferson, NC: McFarland, 2008.

McDonnell, Chris. ed., *The Football Game I'll Never Forget: 100 NFL Stars' Stories.* New York: Firefly Books, 2004.

McGinn, Bob. *The Ultimate Super Bowl Book: A Complete Reference to the Stats, Stars, and Stories Behind Football's Biggest Game—and Why the Best Team Won.* Minneapolis, MN: MVP Books, 2009.

McMillen, Neil R. *Dark Journey: Black Mississippians in the Age of Jim Crow.* Urbana: University of Illinois Press, 1990.

———. *The Citizens' Council: Organized Resistance to the Second Reconstruction, 1954–1964.* Urbana: University of Illinois Press, 1971.

Morris, Willie. *The Courting of Marcus Dupree.* New York: Doubleday, 1983.

Oshinsky, David M. *"Worse Than Slavery": Parchman Farm and the Ordeal of Jim Crow Justice.* New York: Simon and Schuster, 1996.

Payton, Walter, and Don Yaeger. *Never Die Easy: The Autobiography of Walter Payton.* New York: Vintage, 2000.

Pearlman, Jeff. *Sweetness: The Enigmatic Life of Walter Payton.* New York: Gotham Books, 2011.

Pennington, Richard. *Breaking the Ice: The Racial Integration of Southwest Conference Football.* Jefferson, NC: McFarland, 1987.

Percy, William Alexander. *Lanterns on the Levee: Recollections of a Planter's Son.* Baton Rouge: Louisiana State University Press, 1973. First published 1941 by Knopf.

Perkins, John. *Let Justice Roll Down: John Perkins Tells His Own Story.* Glendale, CA: G/L Publications, 1971.

Perrin, Tom. *Football: A College History.* Jefferson, NC: McFarland, 1987.

Phillips, Michael. *White Metropolis: Race, Ethnicity, and Religion in Dallas, 1841–2001.* Austin: University of Texas Press, 2006.

Pickett, Al. *The Greatest Texas Sports Stories You've Never Heard.* Abilene, TX: State House Press, 2007.

Poussaint, Alvin F. "Sex and the Black Male." *Ebony* 27 (August 1972): 114–20.

Powdermaker, Hortense. *After Freedom: A Cultural Study in the Deep South.* New York: Atheneum, 1969.

Rhoden, William C. *Forty Million Dollar Slaves: The Rise, Fall, and Redemption of the Black Athlete.* New York: Three Rivers Press, 2006.

Roberts, Randy. *Joe Louis.* New Haven, CT: Yale University Press, 2010.

———. *Papa Jack: Jack Johnson and the Era of White Hopes.* New York: Free Press, 1983.

Robinson, Edward J. *The Fight Is On in Texas: A History of African American Churches of Christ, 1865–2000.* Abilene, TX: Abilene Christian University Press, 2008.

Ross, Charles K. *Outside the Lines: African Americans and the Integration of the National Football League.* New York: New York University Press, 1999.

Ross, Charles K., ed. *Race and Sport: The Struggle for Equality on and off the Field.* Jackson: University Press of Mississippi, 2004.

Shropshire, Kenneth L. *In Black and White: Race and Sports in America.* New York: New York University Press, 1996.

Singletary, Mike, and Jerry Jenkins. *Singletary on Singletary.* Nashville, TN: Thomas Nelson, 1991.

Skates, John Ray. *Mississippi: A Bicentennial History.* New York: W. W. Norton, 1979.

Smith, Maureen M. "Bill Russell: Pioneer and Champion of the Sixties." In *Out of the Shadows: A Biographical History of African American Athletes,* edited by David K. Wiggins, 223–39. Fayetteville: University of Arkansas Press, 2006.

Stevens, John C. *No Ordinary University: The History of a City on a Hill.* Abilene, TX: Abilene Christian University Press, 1998.

Sugarman, Tracy. *Stranger at the Gates: A Summer in Mississippi.* New York: Hill and Wang, 1966.

Towle, Mike. *Roger Staubach: Captain America.* Nashville, TN: Cumberland House, 2002.

Tye, Larry. *Satchel: The Life and Times of an American Legend.* New York: Random House, 2009.

Ward, Geoffrey C. *Unforgivable Blackness: The Rise and Fall of Jack Johnson.* New York: A. A. Knopf, 2004.

Whittingham, Richard. *What Bears They Were: Chicago Bears Greats Talk about Their Teams, Their Coaches, and the Times of Their Lives,* rev ed. Chicago: Triumph Books, 2002.

Wiggins, David K. *Glory Bound: Black Athletes in a White America.* Syracuse, NY: Syracuse University Press, 1997.

———. " 'Great Speed But Little Stamina:' The Historical Debate over Black Athletic Superiority." *Journal of Sport History* 16 (Summer 1989): 158–85.

———. *Out of the Shadows: A Biographical History of African American Athletes.* Fayetteville: University of Arkansas Press, 2006.

Wilkerson, Isabel. *The Warmth of Other Suns: The Epic Story of America's Great Migration.* New York: Vintage, 2010.

Willis, Arthur C. *Cecil's City: A History of Blacks in Philadelphia, 1638–1979.* New York: Carlton Press, 1990.

Wright, Richard. "The Ethics of Living Jim Crow, An Autobiographical Sketch." In *The Norton Anthology of African-American Literature,* edited by Henry Louis Gates Jr. and Nellie Y. McKay, 1388–96. New York: W. W. Norton, 1997.

Zang, David W. *Fleet Walker's Divided Heart: The Life of Baseball's First Black Major Leaguer.* Lincoln: University of Nebraska Press, 1995.

Gallaway, Steven Kent. "A History of the Desegregation of the Public Schools in Abilene, Texas, During the Wells Administration, 1954–1970." EdD diss., Texas Tech University, 1994.

Gillespie, Deanna M. "'They Walk, Talk, and Act Like New People': Black Women and the Citizenship Education Program, 1957–1970." PhD diss., Binghamton University, 2008.

Mizelle, Richard McKinley, Jr. "Blackwater Blues: The 1927 Flood Disaster, Race, and the Remaking of Regional Identity, 1900–1930." PhD diss., Rutgers University, 2006.

Moye, Joseph Todd. "'Sick and Tired of Being Sick and Tired': Social Origins and Consequences of the Black Freedom Struggle in Sunflower County, 1945–1986." PhD diss., University of Texas, 1999.

Nightingale, Carl Husemoller. "'It Makes Me Wonder How I Keep from Going Under': Young People in Poor Black Philadelphia, and the Formation of a Collective Experience, 1940–1990." PhD diss., Princeton University, 1992.

Simmons, Sallie Anne. "Attitudes Toward School Consolidation in a Mississippi Delta Town." MS thesis, Delta State University, 2006.

Tisdale, John R. "Medgar Evers (1925–1963) and the Mississippi Press." PhD diss., University of North Texas, 1996.

Wood, Spencer D. "The Roots of Black Power: Land, Civil Society, and the State in Mississippi Delta, 1935–1968." PhD diss., University of Wisconsin–Madison, 2006.

Index